WONGTIN

Your Chinese Horoscope
for the Year of the

SNAKE

January 24th 2001 to February 11th 2002

Asia 2000 Ltd & Maison d'éditions Quaille
Hong Kong

© 2000 Maison d'éditions Quaille

ISBN 962-7160-96-2

Published by Asia 2000 Ltd
http://www.asia2000.com.hk/

Printed in 2000 in Hong Kong by Editions Quaille ltd.

PREFACE

I went with Master WONG Tin to visit a place that was supposed to be the house of the famous Kung Fu Wing Chun Boxer, Master YIP Man in Fushan, China, near Guanzhou. The government now classifies this house, "The Home of Kip" as a protected historical site.

If a location is situated in a position that warrants good energy, the people within that space will be affected in their life by that good energy, according to Fung Shui theory. During this trip to "The Home of Kip" I asked Master Wong whether this place had the energy to create a famous Kung Fu man. Master Wong immediately pulled out his Fung Shui compass to assess the energy for that location. To my great surprise, Master Wong said "The Home of Yip" did not have the energy to create a boxer, but instead the energy for a literate man.

What a travesty! Why was "The Home of Yip" not the house of Master YIP Man? After I investigated, I realized there are two places called "The Home of Yip" and we were at the wrong one.

After that experience, I realized the great power of Fung Shui, and of Master Wong Tin.

Master Wong Tin has been studying and practicing Fung Shui for more than thirty years. His profound knowledge in the field includes theories that fit the needs of people in contemporary societies. He is a quiet man and a modest man that does not like to be the star of the show. With great expectations from his friends and acquaintances, Master Wong Tin presents Your Chinese Horoscopes: For the Year of the Snake 2001.

I invite you to explore your horoscopes with Master Wong Tin, and I wish you luck in the Year of the Snake 2001.

Leung Ting

Leung Ting is a master of Wing Chun. He studied under the Grandmaster Yip Man.

WONG TIN

Master Wong Tin has been studying and practicing Fung Shui for more than thirty years. His profound knowledge in the field includes theories that fit the needs of people in contemporary societies. He is a quiet man and a modest man that does not like to be the star of the show.

止見趙齊禾穗秀　何曾燕楚稻苗勻
而兼蠶婦提筐泣　疾病炎天每及身

辛巳年來高下分　豐凶處處欠平均
依山可望堆場圃　傍水難期滿廩圈

The Year of the Serpent and the Sing（辛）

Will have its ups and downs.

Good and bad will be widely spread.

Near the mountains crops will thrive;

By the rivers only sadness will grow.

The North will prosper

But the South will fail.

The girls tending the silk will be in tears;

And sickness will visit

With the hot days of Summer.

Explaining the Chinese Almanac:

The Chinese Almanac is called the Tong Shu (通書), literally the General Book; but Shu (書) has the same sound as the word for loss (輸). Especially in Southern China, the expression Tong Sheng (通勝), meaning general victory, is usually used. The Chinese Almanac is meant to be a master book predicting all possible events - whether good, bad or fair-, for each day of the year. It is meant to be revised and published annually.

Predictions in the Chinese Almanac or Tong Sheng (通勝) are made from eight vantage points. The first four are the directions of the compass: North, South, East and West. The final four are attitudes of nature: Zoushu (奏書), Boshi (博士), Lishi (力士) and Canshi (蠶室).

Zoushu (奏書): This direction/position represents the God of Fortune (貴神). The God of Fortune is also called the God of Water (水神). It concerns itself with appropriate places for worship for bringing luck and good fortune, also for determining auspicious places for construction or change.

Boshi (博士): This direction/position represents the God of Mercy (善神). The God of Mercy is also called the God of Fire (火神). It concerns itself with benefits that might accrue to an owner, master or boss, and also for determining auspicious moments for change. Boshi

(博士) *interacts directly and contradictorily with Zoushu* (奏書).

Lishi (力士): *This direction/position represents the God of Anger* (惡神). *The God of Anger resembles the guards of the emperor responsible for executing and killing. It concerns itself with sickness and death.*

Canshi (蠶室): *This direction/position represents the God of Danger* (凶神). *It concerns itself with all bad and unfortunate matters, such as funerals, and determines times not suitable for change or renovation. Any violations carry bad effects on harvest and results.*

The diagram shows the directions for the good and the bad of the current year (Year of the Snake)
(流年吉凶方位圖)

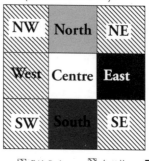

NW	North	NE
West	Centre	East
SW	South	SE

▨ *Excellent*　　▨ *Fairly Good*　　▨ *Acceptable*　　■ *Very bad*

For the current year (流年), *the North and the South are very good, the East is bad and the West is fairly good.*

The eight directions for the good and bad in the Year of the Snake (蛇年):

Excellent	: *The North, The South.*
Fairly Good	: *The West.*
Acceptable	: *SE, NE, SW and NW.*
Very Bad	: *The East.*

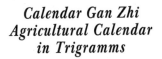

Calendar Gan Zhi
Agricultural Calendar
in Trigramms

In China you can find three kinds of calendars: solar, lunar and Gan Zhi, which means agricultural calendar.

The agricultural calendar includes the following months:

☶	1st month (Tiger's month): from the Beginning of Spring to Rain Water
☶	2nd month (Rabbit's month): Awakening from hibernation to the Spring Equinox
☳	3rd month (Dragon's month) : Pure Brightness to Grain Rain
☱	4th month (Snake's month): Beginning of Summer to Grain Full
☱	5th month (Horse's month) : Grain in Ear to the Summer Solstice
☲	6th month (Ram's month): Slight Heat to Great Heat
☰	7th month (Monkey's month) : Beginning of Autumn to the limit of Heat
☴	8th month (Rooster's month) : White Dew to the Autumnal Equinox
☵	9th month (Dog's month) : Cold Dew to First Frost
☷	10th month (Pig's month) : Beginning of Winter to Slight Snow
☷	11th month (Rat's month) : Great Snow to the Winter Solstice
☷	12th month(Ox's month) : Slight Cold to Great Cold

Under the Xia Dynasty (approximately 21 centuries to 18 centuries before Jesus Christ), the month of the Tiger was considered to be the first month of the year.

Under the Shang Dynasty (approximately 18 centuries to 11 centuries before Jesus Christ), the month of the Ox was considered to be the first month of the year.

Under the Zhou Dynasty (approximately 11 centuries to 771 years before Jesus Christ), the month of the Rat was considered to be the first month of the year.

Under the Quing Dynasty (approximately 221 years to 206 years before Jesus Christ), the month of the Tiger was again considered to be the first month of the year, and this has been preserved to the present day. The majority of Geomancians and fortunetellers use this calendar in their calculations. For example, if a person is born on January 30th, this corresponds with the 7th of the first month of the Snake year. As Spring starts on February 4th, that person belongs to the Dragon year and not to the Snake year.

CONTENT

I. General account of the Horoscope for the Year 2001

Rat 8
Ox 14
Tiger 21
Rabbit 28
Dragon 35
Snake 42
Horse 49
Ram 56
Monkey 63
Rooster 70
Dog 77
Pig 84

II. General Prospects for the 12 Signs by month

Rat 92
Ox 99
Tiger 106
Rabbit 115
Dragon 123
Snake 131
Horse 140
Ram 148
Monkey 156
Rooster 165
Dog 173
Pig 181

Annexes

Almanac 190
Dates of Lunar Years 217
Predicting the Sex of a Child 221
Months of the Snake Year 222

I.

Generoal Account
of the Horoscope
for the Year 2001

RAT

Prospects for those born in the Year of the Rat

1912, 1924, 1936, 1948, 1960, 1972, 1984, 1996

People born in the Year of the Rat have three auspicious stars shining overhead: Ziwei (紫微)(Purple Delicate), Longde (龍德)(Dragon Virtue) and Wenchang (文昌)(Literary Prosperity). When auspicious stars shine, there will be help from sages and luck will proliferate. This will facilitate the seeking of wealth and everything will go smoothly as wished. When Ziwei shines, luck will be plentiful and will bring huge wealth and great honor. When Longde shines, there will be help from sages and everything will go smoothly as wished. Longde ensures protection and brings peace and safety. When Wenchang shines, literary ability will be enhanced and great progress in learning is expected.

But people born in the Year of the Rat may also have two inauspicious stars this year: Tian'e (天厄) (Heaven Disaster) and Baobai (暴敗) (Violent Defeat). With Tian'e, nothing planned will be accomplished, and diseases may be prevalent. With Baobai, it is easy to get into quarrels and troubles. However, if there are auspicious stars coming to their rescue, there should be no great problems.

This year promises good prospects and the good luck of last year may continue for people born in the Year of the Rat. But this good and on-going luck will gradually decline towards the end of the year.

As far as career is concerned, those born in the Year of the Rat may rise head and shoulders above others in competition, but their rivals will not give up readily. Therefore, morale must be kept high at every moment. This year, staying in their present post will allow more opportunities for success than going through a work transfer.

In terms of wealth, funds will circulate smoothly bringing good prospects for their career.

Prospects in love present happiness for the dating pair. With the help of their friends, single people may make new friends.

As for family, problems can only be solved with better communication when disagreements occur between husband and wife, and family members on issues such as children's education.

In terms of health, it is advised to pay attention to health programs and the news to obtain more knowledge about health and how to put it into practice. There will be no big problems in health throughout the whole year.

People born in the Year of the Rat are serious and diligent in their work, and ready to lend a helping hand to others. So they are quite popular, and can get along with others very well. Most people will find those born in the Year of the Rat lovely and charming, and will not dislike them. The character of those born in the Year of the Rat will generally bring them happiness when they marry those women born in years of other signs.

Females born in the Year of the Rat are tender and good hearted, and are typical of well-educated maidens with sweet smiles from families of distinction; very much appreciated by men. But females born in the Year of the Rat must pay due attention to their marriage prospects.

With a proper marriage, those born in the Year of the Rat will have a steady and harmonious marriage. They will have a nice family with much love; the elderly will be respected and children will be taken good care of.

Those born in the Year of the Rat will have SUPER LUCK when marrying those born in the years of the Ox, Dragon and Monkey; they will have LUCK if they marry those born in the years of the Rat, Tiger,

Snake, Dog and Pig; they will have HALF ILL LUCK when they marry those born in the years of the Rabbit, Ram and Rooster; and they will have ILL LUCK when they marry those born in the Year of the Horse.

The prospects of marriage for those born in the Year of the Rat:

Auspicious: promise from the bottom of one's heart, which is the manifestation of the greatest luck; they will have wealth, honor, fortune, success and happiness follow them all through their lives.

Inauspicious: no way to get rich, and disasters may even make it difficult for them to establish their careers and families.

General prospects for those born in the Year of the Rat

Born in 1912 (壬子 renzi), 90-year-olds:
Those born in 1912 must be very careful when moving about to avoid limb injuries.

Auspicious Numbers: 8 & 9 for males; and 1, 8, & 9 for females.

Born in 1924 (甲子 jiazi), 78-year-olds:
The elderly born in 1924 are generally in good health. They may have a very pleasant year if they are not too stubborn in attitude, if they do not have wild flights of fancy and if they take good care when moving around. They should not live alone to avoid danger.

Auspicious Numbers: 1 & 4 for males; and 1 & 4 for females.

Born in 1936 (丙子 bingzi), 66-year-olds:

Those born in 1936 may have a fortune star shining overhead this year with normal and extra income flowing in with great ease. But to avoid a turn to poverty, they should not be too greedy. They may enjoy great popularity and help from friends.

Auspicious Numbers: 1 & 7 for males; and 1, 7, & 8 for females.

Born in 1948 (戊子 wuzi), 54-year-olds:

There will be an ideal income for those born in 1948 this year. However, they had better not lend money to, or provide a guarantee for others. It is better to refrain from speculation and gambling. The business will have to go through a cautious and steady development, and the handling of everything between husband and wife should focus on harmony.

Auspicious Numbers: 5, 7 & 8 for males; and 5 & 6 for females.

Born in 1960 (庚子 gengzi), 42-year-olds:

Those born in 1960 may experience some ups and downs this year. It will be difficult to accumulate money and wealth. They may, however, have some achievements in their career. They should take the initiative and not let other swift-footed individuals leave them behind. They should guard against others robbing them of their achievements.

Auspicious Numbers: 1, 7 & 8 for males; and 7 & 8 for females.

Born in 1972 (壬子 *renzi*), 30-year-olds:

Those born in 1972 may have a stream of inspiration and good advances in work, but they should understand that more gains come from more work, and should not pin their hopes on sheer luck. They must take great care and pains in their business decisions, and they should carefully guard business secrets or they may suffer defeat on the verge of victory.

Auspicious Numbers: 1, 9 for males; and 1, 8 & 9 for females.

Born in 1984 (甲子 *jiazi*), 18-year-olds:

Those born in 1984 are good at literary thinking. They may have ideal results if they work hard in their studies. Their parents should pay attention to all kinds of temptations in everyday life, including the pursuit of famous brands and sex. But they are not very good in health, and care must be exercised so it does not affect their studies. Their parents must be very careful in giving them instructions.

Auspicious Numbers: 1 & 8 for males; and 1, 8 & 9 for females.

Born in 1996 (丙子 *bingzi*), 6-year-olds:

Children born in 1996 are in better health than last year except for occasional ailments. Parents should explore their talents in music so that they may develop healthy interests.

Auspicious Numbers: 6 & 7 for males; and 6 & 7 for females.

OX

Prospects for those born in the Year of the Ox

1913, 1925, 1937, 1949, 1961, 1973, 1985, 1997

People born in the Year of the Ox may have Huagai (華蓋) (Canopy), an auspicious star shining over them, which will allow them to write articles of super quality, and have excellent results on tests and exams. This will give them great fame and honor. It is said disasters may turn into good luck when you have a good reputation and power.

Meanwhile, three inauspicious stars will shine: Baihu (白虎)(White Tiger), Huangfan (黃幡)(Yellow Banner) and Tianku (天哭) (Heaven Wail). If those born in the Year of the Ox stay calm and cool with a fair and just attitude while facing cer-

tain unfavorable situations, there may be an auspicious star that comes to their rescue.

Those born in the Year of the Ox may have plain sailing this year, because of the 'Three Harmonies' between their prospects and the prospects of those born in the Year of the Snake.

There may be some new opportunities and developments for those who have been in a rather low mood and those who have been wondering about the necessity of changing their present situation. These people should find the courage and have confidence in themselves.

For those born in the Year of the Ox, the key point is to broaden relationships with other people that are beneficial to them. Moreover, this is a very important preparatory year for the future.

In terms of career, promotion is not a whimsical dream. Personal efforts and career prospects may be complementary to one another in producing ideal results. They should not get bogged down because of things that happened in the past.

As far as their luck in making money is concerned, they may have extra income, but wealth comes easy and goes quickly. Special attention should be paid to sensible thrift and the expense of socializing.

The prospects in love show a commingled situation with both departure and new chances, yet nothing promises a definite expectation. The love they in-

tend to give up should be handled with resolution and they should try to get ready for the new love.

As for family there may be some unexpected events and disputes that will cause a chain reaction. They should try not to be too stubborn and narrow-minded.

Regarding health, due attention should be paid to physical exhaustion caused by overwork and injury. They should also guard against liver, head and heart diseases, as well as old illnesses that have plagued them.

Males born in the Year of the Ox are steady in character and inarticulate in expression. Their cold appearance lacks a sense of humor. They are relatively introverted, but deep down they are warm and wise. It is such serious, cool and polite appearances that win many warm and extroversive female's hearts.

Females born in the Year of the Ox are virtuous, diligent and faithful in their love, and they will keep the family in good order. They are good wives and mothers in the minds of the males.

People born in the Year of the Ox may lead a warm, happy and content family life if they make a good match in marriage. They may be loyal to their family, and love and protect their kin and children.

Those born in the Year of the Ox will have SU-PER LUCK when marrying those born in the years

of the Rat, Snake and Rooster; they will have LUCK if they marry those born in the years of the Ox, Tiger, Rabbit, Monkey and Pig; they will have HALF ILL LUCK when they marry those born in the years of the Dragon, Horse and Dog; and they will have ILL LUCK when they marry those born in the Year of the Ram.

The prospects of marriage for those born in the Year of the Ox:

Auspicious: fortunate marriage endowed by heaven, and the family will enjoy a good reputation and wealth; just, kind and gentle in character, their family may enjoy great prosperity with good luck, stability and virtue all their lives.

Inauspicious: good luck is accompanied by bad luck, with happiness followed by bitterness, thus a combination of joy and poverty; there is happiness in the first half of their life, but there is no sign of enterprise shown on their part; inward worries and bitterness will lead to a final doom.

General prospects for those born in the Year of the Ox

Born in 1913 (癸丑 guichou), 89-year-olds:

Those people born in 1913 have good health and luck but it is easy for them to suffer from ailments. They must be careful while walking lest they should fall down.

Auspicious Numbers: 0 & 7 for males; and 0 & 7 for females.

Born in 1925 (乙丑 yichou), 77-year-olds:

Those elderly people born in 1925 may enjoy a leisurely life this year. They just have to pay attention to the safety of their house, and they should not lend money to others. They will have a happy year.

Auspicious Numbers: 2 & 8 for males; and 1, 2 & 8 for females.

Born in 1937 (丁丑 dingchou), 65-year-olds:

Those born in 1937 may have quite good moods and states of mind; humorous character facilitates their contact with others. But they should take notice and good care of their increasing ailments.

Auspicious Numbers: 4 & 9 for males; and 6 & 7 for females.

Born in 1949 (己丑 jichou), 53-year-olds:

Those born in 1949 may have twists and turns in their business development this year. If they work in a down-to-earth way and keep a low profile, they will gradually enter a favorable situation. However, it is easy for them to act emotionally. The offer of a great and sympathetic hand to help others may invite misunderstanding and criticism, which will turn good luck to bad luck, and lead to failure in their work.

Auspicious Numbers: 1, 6 & 7 for males; and 6 & 7 for females.

Born in 1961 (辛丑 xinchou), 41-year-olds:

Those born in 1961 may face a great challenge in career, and they may have no bad luck if they have no excessive demands or greed. In terms of emotions, there will be bewildering labyrinths, but potential solutions also exist.

Auspicious Numbers: 8 & 9 for males; and 1, 7 & 8 for females.

Born in 1973 (癸丑 guichou), 29-year-olds:

Those born in 1973 may experience a complicated and unpredictable relationship, only mutual understanding and concession may help solve serious problems. There will be good luck with normal income, but it is easy to lose money and wealth. There will be some profits through business cooperation with their partners. They should be cautious with their finances to guard against economic crisis. They should also stay away from debauchery and guard against dangers caused by water.

Auspicious Numbers: 0, 1 & 9 for males; and 0, 1 & 8 for females.

Born in 1985 (乙丑 *yichou*), 17-year-olds:

Those born in 1985 are traveling in a boat upstream. It is easier to regress than progress. If they can double their efforts and become absorbed in their studies, they will be able to make tremendous progress. They must manage their rebellious spirits.

Auspicious Numbers: 2, 8 & 9 for males; and 2 & 7 for females.

Born in 1997 (丁丑 *dingchou*), 5-year-olds:

Those children born in 1997 should be taken good care of. Everything will be stable except for a few ailments. When playing outdoors they should be well looked after to avoid unexpected accidents.

Auspicious Numbers: 1 & 4 for males; and 1, 4 & 7 for females.

TIGER

Prospects for those born in the Year of the Tiger

1914, 1926, 1938, 1950, 1962, 1974, 1986, 1998

People born in the Year of the Tiger have three auspicious stars: Tiande (天德) (Heaven Virtue), Fuxing (福星)(Fortune Star) and Tianyi (天乙) (Heaven Second). The arrival of auspicious stars will bring success and wealth. Tiande will help in the success of everything; and with help from sages anything can be accomplished.

Nonetheless, those born in the Year of the Tiger also have four inauspicious stars: Jiesha(劫煞) (Robber Killer), Liuhai (Six Pests)(六害), Juanshe (捲舌)(Rolling Tongue) and Jiaosha (絞煞) (Hanging Killer) in front. As long as

they guard against arrogance rather than riding on a high Horse, they should have no great problems and the auspicious stars will come to their rescue.

The year 2001 is a Xinsi (辛巳) year. The Tiger (寅 Yin) is of the nature of the springwood, while the Snake (巳si) is of the nature of early summer, so the two are in conflict against each other. The prospects of the wood nature are weakened due to the burning of fire, thus unable to show the nature of power and decisiveness.

For this reason, for those born in the Tiger year, this will be a year with an alternation of both good and bad lucks, with unbelievably strong prospects while in a favorable horoscope. But when in a weak luck force, they will have a sense of powerlessness no matter how hard they pursue their ideals.

However, those born in the Year of the Tiger are characterized by perseverance, and so long as they maintain stability in spirit and in mood, they will be able to stick it out.

In terms of career, this will be a period of great fluctuations. They should try to avoid being influenced by circumstances by developing good judgment and the ability to correctly grasp the present situation through observation.

As far as luck in making money is concerned,

they will be more sensitive and will no longer get bogged down in squandering and waste, thus accumulating certain wealth.

In love affairs, they are prone to be self-centered and will neglect the feelings of their partners. On the other hand, a passionate pursuit by one side may cause the antipathy from the other side, so it is important to stick to the principle of self-discipline.

In family life, self-centeredness may cause dissatisfaction of family members. But so long as they sincerely express their own feelings, family members may forgive them.

Regarding health, it is most important to reduce pressure. A spiritual exhaustion and too many worries may cause diseases.

Males born in the Tiger year are enthusiastic and optimistic, so they easily attract people of the opposite sex. Those born in the Tiger year will take the initiative in courting the intended partner they love, but sometimes at the critical moment they will appear indecisive and lose good opportunities.

Females born in the Year of the Tiger are independent and eager to do well in everything, and they will not willingly stay at home. They are devoted and dedicated to their career with outstanding achievements. They are the epitome

of the term: Women with power.

When well matched in marriage, those born in the Tiger year will have a happy, rich and fortunate family.

Those born in the Year of the Tiger will have SUPER LUCK when matched in marriage with those born in the years of the Horse and Dog; they will have LUCK if matched in marriage with those born in the years of the Rat, Ox, Tiger, Rabbit, Dragon, Ram, Rooster and Pig; they will have HALF ILL LUCK when they marry those born in the Year of the Snake; and they will have ILL LUCK when they marry those born in the Year of the Monkey.

The prospects of marriage for those born in the Year of the Tiger:

Auspicious: husband and wife are always of one heart; ever-increasing reverence and fame lead to great achievements: wealth, honor and glory, and a great fortune with good luck and longevity; descendents will enjoy great prosperity.

Inauspicious: husband and wife are in conflict against each other; worries upon worries with no hope of success but only the stress of defeat and ruin; no way to dispel the sense of emptiness and loneliness; suffering from injuries and diseases, thus an untimely death.

General prospects for those born in the Year of the Tiger

Born in 1914 (甲寅 *jiayin*), 88-year-olds:

The elderly people born in 1914 are not very good in health, and there may be some ailments. Please give heed to health, and take good care.

Auspicious Numbers: 8 & 9 for males; and 1 & 7 for females.

Born in 1926 (丙寅 *bingyin*), 76-year-olds:

The elders born in 1926 should be careful and cautious when going about or up and down stairs. It is easy for them to suffer limb injuries; care must be taken. They should not move around as much and should seek early treatments of their ailments; they should not take any chances.

Auspicious Numbers: 7 & 8 for males; and 8 & 9 for females.

Born in 1938 (戊寅 *wuyin*), 64-year-olds:

The elderly born in 1938 had better do some proper work or take walks in flower gardens and woods, because the fresh air and verdant landscape may reduce their chances of getting angry. They should not be depressed by problems pertaining to children.

Auspicious Numbers: 1, 4 & 8 for males; and 8 & 9 for females.

Born in 1950 (庚寅 *gengyin*), 52-year-olds:

People born in 1950 must understand self-protection this year because there are many ill-spirited characters. They should be extremely careful with their closest kin, for it is easy to be betrayed or affected by them, thus suffering a tragic loss or even getting involved with a lawsuit.

Auspicious Numbers: 8 & 9 for males; and 1, 4 & 7 for females.

Born in 1962 (壬寅 *renyin*), 40-year-olds:

Those born in 1962 must first of all set a goal for this year's endeavor; aimlessly and recklessly going about things will make the matter even worse. There is no sign of improvement in terms of their marriage or relationship, and they must seek mutual understanding and concession to avoid the rupture in feelings that will lead to divorce.

Auspicious Numbers: 1, 4 & 8 for males; and 8 & 9 for females.

Born in 1974 (甲寅 *jiayin*), 28-year-olds:

Those born in 1974 must prepare for work early this year because storms may come any minute. They should never offend mean people, and they should try to put aside money for unexpected needs. They are healthy, but they should take care not to catch diseases from their food or drink. In business they should be as lenient and tolerant as they possibly can to assure they will not be utterly isolated.

Auspicious Numbers: 7 & 8 for males; and 7 & 8 for females.

Born in 1986 (丙寅 bingyin), 16-year-olds:

Those born in 1986 are very perceptive, yet it is easy for them to be influenced by bad friends, thus losing interest in their studies. They must improve their situation and stay away from mean fellows. Otherwise, they will regress in their studies and go astray.

Auspicious Numbers: 1, 4 & 7 for males; and 1, 4 & 8 for females.

Born in 1998 (戊寅 wuyin), 4-year-olds:

Children born in 1998 are basically healthy except for a few ailments. It is not proper to leave them alone at home or let them go out and play on their own, because there might be some unexpected accidents.

Auspicious Numbers: 1 & 8 for males; and 8 & 9 for females.

RABBIT

Prospects for those born in the Year of the Rabbit

1915, 1927, 1939, 1951, 1963, 1975, 1987, 1999

People born in the Year of the Rabbit have four inauspicious stars overhead this year: Tiango (天狗)(Sky Dog), Diaoke(弔客) (Guest Hanger), Zaisha(災煞) (Ferocious Killer) and Qiuyu(囚獄) (Prison Convict). However, they should not go panicking, because misfortune may turn into good luck so long as they are cautious and develop endurance that may help them get out of a predicament safely.

The Rabbit is of the wood nature. Because the

Snake of the twelve animals representing the twelve Earthly Branches is of the fire nature, the two are sympathetic to each other and have a good relationship. For this reason, although there are four inauspicious stars coming along, the prospects of those born in the Year of the Rabbit will turn gradually for the better so long as they make proper assessments of circumstances.

Those born in the Year of the Rabbit will achieve good results so long as they go steadily towards their set goal. This is also a year during which happy events will take place one after another. But the apprehension is that the negative influence of last year may bring them back to the shadow of passive depression if they don't have a positive attitude and a definite aim.

In terms of career, self-employed people may have fairly good business operations. But it is better not to get into speculation or gambling. Employees can try to bring their potential ability into full play, and they may have the chance for a rise in pay.

Their luck in making money is generally good, and occasionally they may get unexpected benefits from investment or speculation. But when they have the profits, they must remember to stop at an appropriate point.

In love affairs they will have good opportunities

to enjoy companions of the opposite sex. Females, especially, may have many more chances to be invited out by males. And some friends may also introduce them to male friends. Those who have partners already may decide on their marriage.

As for family life, there will be a very harmonious atmosphere.

Regarding health, they will generally have no problems, but they should not bite more than they can chew.

Those born in the Year of the Rabbit are gentle, kind and polite, paying due attention to their appearances. They are in possession of a special charm, which attracts the attention of the opposite sex anyplace. Males born in the Rabbit year should marry those virtuous, quiet, well-educated and beautiful females with good interest and taste. Females born in the Rabbit year are tender, considerate and compassionate. So they should marry those gentle, generous, humorous, enterprising and successful males.

With a proper match in marriage, people born in the Rabbit year may enjoy a colorful, romantic and profound family life with mutual help and affection.

Those born in the Year of the Rabbit will have

SUPER LUCK when marrying those born in the years of the Ram, Dog and Pig; they will have LUCK if they marry those born in the years of the Ox, Tiger, Rabbit, Snake and Monkey; they will have HALF ILL LUCK when they marry those born in the years of the Rat, Dragon and Horse; and they will have ILL LUCK when they marry those born in the Year of the Rooster.

The prospects of marriage for those born in the Year of the Rabbit:

Auspicious: their career promises success just as the phoenix is ready to fly; the peaceful enjoyment of respect and glory, and marginal profits indicate great promise; cautious actions may bring about security and prosperity.

Inauspicious: hardly any family happiness; always in adversity; career unsuccessful with no good luck; poverty and obstacles; lack of fighting spirits; misfortunes and disasters come one after another; a taste of various pains and agonies.

31

General prospects for those born in the Year of the Rabbit

Born in 1915 (乙卯 yimao), 87-year-olds:

The elderly people born in 1915 may generally enjoy good health, but they should be extremely careful while taking a walk.

Auspicious Numbers: 7, 8 & 9 for males; and 7, 8 & 9 for females.

Born in 1927 (丁卯 dingmao), 75-year-olds:

The elderly born in 1927 are generally in a good mood, but there will be some ailments. They should pay attention to food.

Auspicious Numbers: 4 & 7 for males; and 1, 4 & 7 for females.

Born in 1939 (己卯 jimao), 63-year-olds:

Those born in 1939 are generally in good health and good mood this year.

Auspicious Numbers: 6 & 9 for males; and 1, 6 & 8 for females.

Born in 1951 (辛卯 xinmao), 51-year-olds:

Those born in 1951 have a year of both good and ill luck. So long as they do not cherish too high an expectation, it will be a rather good year. Nevertheless, they should do everything with great care,

and solid work is necessary rather than impatient anxiety. They should understand that good harvests are usually obtained through efforts.

Auspicious Numbers: 1, 8 & 9 for males; and 6 & 8 for females.

Born in 1963 (癸卯 *guimao*), 39-year-olds:

Those born in 1963 will have a successful career and good health, but it is easy to get involved in interpersonal troubles and strife. They must try to improve their interpersonal relations with others; otherwise their efforts will prove futile. They should not be too greedy about side income. And they should remember not to lend to, or borrow from others. And they should not serve as warrantors.

Auspicious Numbers: 8, 0 & 1 for males; and 8 & 0 for females.

Born in 1975 (乙卯 *yimao*), 27-year-olds:

Those born in 1975 may experience emotional and complicated upheavals. They should not get indulged in love; otherwise their career might be affected. For this reason, they must remain calm. They are generally in good health except for some troubles with oral diseases.

Auspicious Numbers: 1, 7 & 8 for males; and 7 & 8 for females.

Born in 1987 (丁卯 dingmao), 15-year-olds:

Children born in 1987 have pretty good luck, but it is easy for them to be burdensome. They should develop a sharp eye to recognize people of various types and they should take care not to be bullied by villains or it will lead to great troubles. They should seek timely advice from their guardians or elders, and they should guard against unexpected accidents. They should not forget the saying: extreme joy may beget sorrow.

Auspicious Numbers: 4 & 8 for males; and 1, 4 & 8 for females.

Born in 1999 (乙卯 yimao), 15-year-olds:

Little children born in 1999 are basically healthy, but small diseases may often occur, such as bronchitis.

Auspicious Numbers: 6 & 9 for males; and 1 & 8 for females.

DRAGON

Prospects for those born in the Year of the Dragon

1916, 1928, 1940, 1952, 1964, 1976, 1988, 2000

People born in the Year of the Dragon have two lucky stars coming along this year: Tianxi (天喜)(Heaven Joy) and Tangfu (唐符) (Grand Auspice). The inauspicious stars will include Bingfu (病符) (Disease Symbol), Guasu (Widowed Dwelling), Suisha (歲煞) (Yearly Kill) and Moyue (陌越)(Road Crossing). However, so long as they remain modest and frugal by taking no undue wealth, they will avoid danger.

Those born in the Year of the Dragon will be full of vigor and vitality this year and full of youthful spirits. Active participation may attract attention,

and on that account, self-complacence and unruliness may bring frustrations. So consequently, they must take great care. If they want to succeed, they must be open-minded in taking others' opinions and suggestions. In addition, they should not neglect the importance of a modest and discreet attitude. But most of all they should try to be enterprising.

Younger people are full of vigor and high morale, and will have very great potential achievements while the middle-aged will be fatigued by public duties and personal affairs.

In terms of career, there will be a large workload, almost more than they can bear because of a newly developed business. But good control of the situation and solid effort will obtain recognition from other colleagues and they will make great advances in their work.

Their luck in making money will gradually improve, but the expense of socializing will increase accordingly, hence no considerable wealth can be accumulated. They should avoid extravagance and vanity.

In love affairs the young may have opportunities to get acquainted with new partners, but they must be cautious in their action. For the middle-aged and the elderly, the simpler relations may become rather complicated ones. It is better to have their desires under proper control and avoid extramarital love

affairs. They should put their family first.

In family life they should try to maintain a harmonious atmosphere and guard against quarrels and disputes.

Regarding health they should not be over confident about their physical strength, because they may break down from constant overwork thus doing harm to their health. They must abide by a healthy plan for work and rest.

People born in the Dragon year have a magic charm to attract the opposite sex. But they are usually morally lofty, full of fantasies, proud and straightforward. Those born in the Dragon year are often preoccupied with their own grand and lofty fancies with little time to consider whom they have a fancy for, so they seldom express their affections. Yet when they come across someone of the opposite sex with good upbringing and culture, there will come a natural and ideal marriage.

Though people born in the Dragon year are somewhat conceited, they are sincere and their feelings come from the bottom of their hearts. They are typically unrestrained in personal character; sometimes they might leave their warm and cozy family in order to pursue their dreams, ideals and career.

Females born in the Year of the Dragon are not happy with an unknown life, and they are devoted

to their work. They will compete with males in career. They have the quality of women with tough will and power.

If they are well matched in marriage, those born in the Dragon year may enjoy a happy and perfectly satisfactory family life.

Those born in the Year of the Dragon will have SUPER LUCK when matched in marriage with those born in the years of the Rat, Monkey and Rooster; they will have LUCK if matched in marriage with those born in the years of the Tiger, Snake, Horse, Ram and Pig; they will have HALF ILL LUCK when they marry those born in the years of the Ox, Rabbit and Dragon; and they will have ILL LUCK when they marry those born in the Year of the Dog.

The prospects of marriage for those born in the Year of the Dragon:

Auspicious: accompanied with fortune and fame, full of wisdom and courage; resolute in will; good and ideal marriage, rich and successful, industrious and frugal in work and career; more prosperous in old age; fortune and reputation handed down from generation to generation.

Inauspicious: no harmony between husband and wife, which will lead to divorce; broken down family with husband forsaking the wife; family misfortune, hard and complicated fate; inviting misfortunes and disasters; plagued with worries.

General prospects for those born in the Year of the Dragon

Born in 1916 (丙辰 bingchen), 86-year-olds:

The elderly people born in 1916 are generally in pretty good moods, but are slightly poor in health. For this reason, they should take care not to get injured by fall.

Auspicious Numbers: 3 & 9 for males; and 3 & 9 for females.

Born in 1928 (戊辰 wuchen), 74-year-olds:

The elderly born in 1928 should by no means get angry, because anger may affect their health. They should be broad-minded about everything, and try to keep themselves in a cheerful mood by letting others take care of things. They should also be careful when moving about.

Auspicious Numbers: 5, 8 & 9 for males; and 5 & 9 for females.

Born in 1940 (庚辰 gengchen), 62-year-olds:

People born in 1940 are in fairly good health. They should be forbearing and conciliatory with family members; they should not get irritated. However, they have too many worries at heart and should be on guard against being tricked by others.

Auspicious Numbers: 7 & 8 for males; and 7 & 8 for females.

Born in 1952 (壬辰 renchen), 50-year-olds:

Those born in 1952 have good luck, thus they may as well put forward some investments. They may have a trial in lottery and it might bring them good luck, but it is not proper for them to speculate. In addition, they must try to be forbearing when dealing with people, and they should never act on impulse, or it will be hard for them to have any close friends.

Auspicious Numbers: 8 & 9 for males; and 9 for females.

Born in 1964 (甲辰 jiachen), 38-year-olds:

Those born in 1964 have rather good luck this year. Even if they have troubles or obstacles in their way, they will be able to solve the problems through their own wisdom and efforts. Nonetheless, they should never touch gambling or get engaged in speculation or profiteering because it might lead them towards danger.

Auspicious Numbers: 1 & 7 for males; and 1 & 9 for females.

Born in 1976 (丙辰 *bingchen), 26-year-olds:*

Those born in 1976 may have moderate luck in making money this year, however this requires hard work. There should be some achievements in work and financial gains as well. Married people should pay attention to undue love affairs this year, otherwise they may bring about disasters. When signing a contract in business, they should pay double attention to the details, and in terms of health they should be on guard against epidemics.

Auspicious Numbers: 3, 8 & 9 for males; and 3, 8 & 9 for females.

Born in 1988 (戊辰 *wuchen), 14-year-olds:*

Young friends born in 1988 may have better luck in studies than last year, but they are prone to go off into wild flights of fancy. Their parents should come to their rescue, which may help them improve their grades in school.

Auspicious Numbers: 5 & 9 for males; and 5 & 9 for females.

Born in 2000 (庚辰 *gengchen), 2-year-olds:*

Children born in 2000 are generally happy and it is easy to look after them, but care must be taken not to let them catch bronchitis.

Auspicious Numbers: 7 & 8 for males; and 7 & 8 for females.

SNAKE

Prospects for those born in the Year of the Snake

1905, 1917, 1929, 1941, 1953, 1965, 1977, 1989

Those born in the Year of the Snake have three auspicious stars shining overhead: Suijia (歲駕)(Yearly Arrival), Tianjie (天解)(Heaven Deliver) and Guoyin(國印) (State Seal); there are also four inauspicious stars: Taisui (太歲)(Jupiter), Fuchen(浮沉) (Oscillater), Jianfeng (劍鋒) (Sword Edge) and Fushi (浮屍) (Prostrate Corpse). There is a saying: The pursuit of fame may bring about profits and diligent study may bring about gains. There is the possibility of offending Taizang (Great Treasure), so caution should be taken

to avoid bloodshed. However, so long as they take precautions in everything they do, and with the help of auspicious stars, they should have no great problems.

Those born in the Year of the Snake should be cautious and tolerant, and seek stability in their life. There will be good fortune in their future, and they will become more active gradually as they focus their attention.

When leading an uneventful life, they may ignore changes in circumstances. If they try to hurt a smart and conspicuous figure, they might get into trouble. Everything in their possession will be uprooted and swept away. They should not be too ambitious because the consequence might be too much for them to handle. They should be modest, and try to have a firm grasp of opportunities for success.

In career they have very good luck and can achieve what they wish. Meanwhile they should not attempt what is beyond their ability and should avoid making decisions all by themselves and acting without consulting others. They should try to achieve harmony with the environment in order to gain success.

In terms of their luck in making money, they should not make great investments just because they have

achieved their goal at a certain stage. They will lead a safe and stable life if they avoid ambitious moments.

In love affairs they will be even closer with their already acquainted partners, and for those who have not been lucky in love affairs, there will be good opportunities. There will be good chances for further development of the relations with their intended sweethearts.

In family there might be some quarrels and disputes, but they should be tolerant and try to solve problems and make peace.

Regarding health, they should pay attention to getting sufficient rest so as not to be exhausted. They should guard against diseases of internal organs and diseases of their past.

People born in the Snake year are clever, articulate, profound in thought, and elegant in conduct and conversation. They are gentle, gorgeous, charming and wise in judgment.

Those born in the Year of the Snake usually will not show an obvious anxiety in love, and sometimes they have a warm heart under a cool and calm appearance. For their intended sweethearts they will not start an immediate courting. They will calmly observe and go through a repeated comparison.

Females born in the Snake year are talented,

calm and insightful, but sometimes they will be affected by emotions.

When well matched in marriage those born in the Snake year will enjoy a happy relationship with a good partner, and both husband and wife will have a good sense of responsibility.

Those born in the Year of the Snake will have SUPER LUCK when matched in marriage with those born in the years of the Ox and Rooster; they will have LUCK if matched in marriage with those born in the years of the Rat, Rabbit, Dragon, Snake, Horse, Ram, Monkey and Dog; they will have HALF ILL LUCK when they marry those born in the year of the Tiger; and they will have ILL LUCK when they marry those born in the Year of the Pig.

The prospects of marriage for those born in the Year of the Dragon:

Auspicious: successes in career through solid work; both fame and fortune; happy and rich all their life.

Inauspicious: family plagued with hardships and frustrations; no tender feelings or real communication between husband and wife; no descendents; disasters and misfortunes will come one after another; no bright prospects about their later life.

General prospects for those born in the Year of the Snake

Born in 1917 (丁巳 dingsi), 85-year-olds:

The elderly people born in 1917 are slightly poor in health, and for this reason, they should take care of their own health and try to be more open-minded. They should let all other things be handled by family members.

Auspicious Numbers: 4 & 8 for males; and 4 & 9 for females.

Born in 1929 (己巳 jisi), 73-year-olds:

The elderly born in 1929 should pay attention to the safety of the family dwelling. It is easy for them to suffer from injuries when they fall down. So they should take great care when moving around.

Auspicious Numbers: 6 & 8 for males; and 6 & 9 for females.

Born in 1941 (辛巳 xinsi), 61-year-olds:

Those born in 1941 should be careful in their movement because they are not very well in health and will experience some ailments. They should guard against serious injuries from falling.

Auspicious Numbers: 8 & 8 for males; and 8 & 9 for females.

Born in 1953 (癸巳 *guisi*), *49-year-olds:*

Those born in 1954 have a fortune star shining bright overhead, which brings them a very good regular income. However, they should not be too greedy about the unexpected wealth. There will be twists and turns. When people seek cooperation from them, they should not be too particular about the immediate gains.

Auspicious Numbers: 0, 10 & 8 for males; and 0, 10 & 9 for females.

Born in 1965 (乙巳 *yisi*), *37-year-olds:*

Those born in 1965 may have a tendency to fly into a rage this year, and they will worry about their children and kinsmen. They should be more open-minded. The best policy is to be more tolerant about everything. It is advised to go out and stay away for the year, but they should not set out before the fourth of February to avoid unexpected accidents.

Auspicious Numbers: 2 & 8 for males; and 2 & 9 for females.

Born in 1977 (丁巳 *dingsi*), *25-year-olds:*

Those born in 1977 have good luck this year,

which is an improvement over last year. Physical and mental work in their careers will bring an ideal return. Although things cannot always conform to their wishes, they will still have easy success. Those who leave their hometown for business should avoid making a show of their wealth.

Auspicious Numbers: 4 & 8 for males; and 4 & 9 for females.

Born in 1989 (己巳 *jisi*), 13-year-olds:

Those born in 1989 have extremely good perception. If their mind and attention are not diverted, they will surely make great advances in their studies. They are, however, still attracted by some temptations, so they should be well instructed.

Auspicious Numbers: 6 & 8 for males; and 6 & 9 for females.

HORSE

Prospects for those born in the Year of the Horse

1906, 1918, 1930, 1942, 1954, 1966, 1978, 1990

People born in the Year of the Horse have three stars shining this year: Taiyang (太陽)(Sun), Yutang (玉堂)(Jade Hall) and Tianchu(天廚) (Heaven Cuisine). With the Sun shining high, sages will come to their help so they can travel in all directions with success in everything they do. And there are also four inauspicious stars: Huiqi (晦氣)(Whammy), Xianchi (鹹池)(Salty Pond), Taohua (桃花) (Peach Blossom) and Niansha(年煞) (Year Killer). As long as they remain modest, guard against arrogance and rashness, avoid disputes and think carefully about every opportunity,

49

with the help of the auspicious stars, they will experience smooth sailing.

For those born in the Horse year, because Wu (午) is of the fire nature with the male principle, while Si (巳) is of the fire nature with the female principle, there is harmony with the male and female principles. Therefore, if they can avoid disputes with others, assume a modest attitude, improve their personal ability and culture, and pay due attention to health, there will be a rather smooth outlook on life.

They should not act with undue haste while dealing with anything this year. Instead, they should wait quietly for the right chance, while reinforcing their own ability and power. And they should not allow obstacles to interrupt their endeavors. Persevering efforts are of ultimate importance.

In career they have self-confidence and sufficient energy, yet they should think three times before taking action.

In terms of making money, they may accumulate a considerable amount of wealth if they practice economy.

In matters of love they may have vehement moments, but the affectionate and tender feelings will last even longer. Those who have passed the usual time for marriage should wait quietly for opportunities that may bring about good marriage.

In dealing with family affairs, they should encourage family members to exercise, and widen the scope of knowledge to improve their abilities.

Regarding health, they should pay attention to blood pressure and diseases in the chest and eyes. Do not neglect diseases of the digestive system.

People born in the Year of the Horse have a strong constitution, and are open minded. They are quick in thinking and fond of freedom, with a character of independence and unrestraint.

They also are tactful, assiduous and have great endurance.

Those born in the Year of the Horse are earnest and anxious in love, and sometimes they will give anything for love. But the quick gain may also vanish easily. For those born in the Horse year, a gradually expressed tender affection may stand the test of time.

Females born in the Year of the Horse are graceful and delicate in manners, fashionable in dress, frank and lively, full of energy and they have the ability to put everything in good order.

When well matched in marriage, those born in the Horse year will be able to lead a dynamic, warm and happy family life.

Those born in the Year of the Horse will have SU-
PER LUCK when matched in marriage with those
born in the years of the Tiger, Ram and Dog; they
will have LUCK if matched in marriage with those
born in the years of the Dragon, Snake, Monkey,
Rooster and Pig; they will have HALF ILL LUCK
when they marry those born in the years of the
Ox, Rabbit and Horse; and they will have ILL
LUCK when they marry those born in the Year of
the Rat.

The prospects of marriage for those born in the
Year of the Horse:

Auspicious: mutual respect for each other; the
purple cloud coming from the east promises riches
and honor; affluent family situation; prosperous
descendants.

Inauspicious: gloomy prospects at the middle age;
a short life with various diseases; no hope for happiness; living with hardship and poverty; loss of
spouse and separation from their children.

General prospects for those born in the Year of the Horse

Born in 1918 (戊午 *wuwu*), 84-year-olds:

The elderly people born in 1918 have very good luck, and if they are not too stubborn they will have a leisurely life. They should pay attention to the safety of family dwelling without going off in wild flights of fancy. This year will prove a smooth passage.

Auspicious Numbers: 5 & 7 for males; and 5 & 7 for females.

Born in 1930 (庚午 *gengwu*), 72-year-olds:

The elderly people born in 1930 are not in very good health. To help them avoid being injured they should not get angry. They should ask others to do the necessary heavy work for them. They should be cautious when moving around.

Auspicious Numbers: 7 & 8 for males; and 7 & 8 for females.

Born in 1942 (壬午 *renwu*), 60-year-olds:

People born in 1942 generally have good luck. They have a solid and steady foundation, however, disputes may often occur at home, which will often make them unhappy. They should be discreet in speech and conduct when dealing with friends.

Auspicious Numbers: 1 & 9 for males; and 1 & 9 for females.

Born in 1954 (甲午 *jiawu*), 48-year-olds:

Those born in 1954 have better luck than last year. They have rather good luck in making money, but they should never speculate, and can avoid robbery by never giving a slight hint of their wealth. And they should not be too greedy because it may hinder their financial development.

Auspicious Numbers: 7 & 8 for males; and 7 & 8 for females.

Born in 1966 (丙午 *bingwu*), 36-year-olds:

Those born in 1966 have good luck in making money and are well equipped to succeed. However, they should never speculate or gamble, and should keep a low profile to avoid trouble. They should not be naive or they may be cheated and will suffer a loss of money. They are not in perfect health, so they have to pay due attention to the care of their stomach and spleen. This year they should not travel far, a quiet observation is better than a rash action.

Auspicious Numbers: 3 & 8 for males; and 3 & 8 for females.

Born in 1978 (戊午 wuwu), 24-year-olds:

Most people born in 1978 have good luck this year, only a few of them have bad luck. As far as emotions are concerned, the situation is complicated and unpredictable. For this reason they have to stay calm, paying due attention to relations with the opposite sex. They are generally in good health, but it is easy for them to catch the flu.

Auspicious Numbers: 5, 7 & 8 for males; and 5, 7 & 8 for females.

Born in 1990 (庚午 gengwu), 12-year-olds:

The young people born in 1990 have good luck. And they will go to a school of a higher grade without difficulty. However their grade is like sailing against the current: difficult to progress but easy to regress. Consequently, they must double their efforts in their studies. And their strong, rebellious character should be corrected.

Auspicious Numbers: 7 & 8 for males; and 7 & 8 for females.

RAM

Prospects for those born in the Year of the Ram

1907, 1919, 1931, 1943, 1955, 1967, 1979, 1991

People born in the Year of the Ram have four inauspicious stars in front this year: Sangmen(喪門) (Stormy Petrel), Yuesha (月煞)(Month Killer), Feilian (飛簾)(Flying Edge) and Baowei(豹尾) (Leopard Tail). However, if they take a defensive stance rather than a rash advance, mishaps may turn into brilliant prospects. It is said that stability is a fortune, and they should aim at a higher goal. At the same time they should guard against bloodshed, thus turning a mishap into a good fortune. And if they try to make steady progress with no impatience and anxiety, their achievements will be great.

Those born in the Ram year will have a smooth and successful Snake year, for the Snake is of the fire nature, which is associated with the female principle, and the Ram is of the earth nature. According to the five practices regarding the male and female principles, fire may generate earth, which makes the Ram and Snake complementary.

Those born in the Year of the Ram have internal fire and they are well known for their calmness and kindness. They are good at analysis, and will often think three times before taking any action. They will have excellent results if they exercise their full potential. The mastery of the internal situation is the key point for the success of their plans.

In their luck of career, they should have a clear objective and work towards the final goal with perseverance. They should listen to advice from others, and guard against being a law unto themselves.

In terms of their luck in making money, there will be no good proportion between their income and expenses in spite of their hard work. Moreover they should avoid speculation and gambling.

In matters of love, they might have many new acquaintances of the opposite sex, but they tend to have no result due to their whimsical mind. Even if they have met an ideal partner, their ef-

forts will usually be spent in vain.

In family life, they are somewhat affected by their mood. It is easy for them to have issues with their family members.

Regarding health they should be aware of a possible heart attack, hypertension and hepatitis, and other ailments caused by exhaustion.

Those born in the Year of the Ram are gentle in character, and kind and sincere towards people. Yet they are relatively dependent, so they love to live with friends and kinsmen. In addition, they are sensitive with perseverance.

When courting females born in the Ram year, people should patiently observe and judge their character, language and soul. They should not give up just because of a temporary rejection. Perseverance will help win love. Once the female born in the Ram year sets her love on a person, she will regard him as very reliable, and will depend on him all her life.

Females born in the Year of the Ram are sentimental and tender; they have faith in love and are loyal to their husbands and families. They help and take care of their husbands, and also teach their children. They are virtuous wives and good mothers.

When well matched in marriage, people born in

the Year of the Ram will have a sweet and cozy family full of tenderness and affection, and a life full of interests and tastes and harmony. Marriage will usually be long and successful; there is no shortage of gold and silver marriages.

Those born in the Ram year will have SUPER LUCK when matched in marriage with those born in the years of the Rabbit, Horse and Pig; they will have LUCK if matched in marriage with those born in the years of the Tiger, Dragon, Snake, Ram, Monkey and Rooster; they will have HALF ILL LUCK when they marry those born in the years of the Rat and Dog; and they will have ILL LUCK when they marry those born in the Year of the Ox.

The prospects of marriage for those born in the Year of the Ram:

Auspicious: harmonious atmosphere at home; pleasant in character; a fortune endowed by nature; great achievements; good health, virtue and reputation; great fortune through great success.

Inauspicious: hardly any happiness in married life; mishaps come one after another; no good income or shelter all their life; loss of spouse or lack of descendants; frequent disasters and rushing about with fatigue.

59

General prospects for those born in the Year of the Ram

Born in 1919 (己未 jiwei), 83-year-olds:

The elderly people born in 1919 should pay attention to the safety of family dwelling, and should also be cautious when moving about. They should pay attention to the pulmonary system, and should be comforted when in a depressed mood.

Auspicious Numbers: 1 & 6 for males; and 6 & 7 for females.

Born in 1931 (辛未 xinwei), 71-year-olds:

The elderly people born in 1931 will be in a good mood this year. They have no ordinary luck. They will have a very plain sailing year so long as they do not attempt any dangerous undertakings and pay close attention to ailments. They should be careful with their diet.

Auspicious Numbers: 7, 8 & 9 for males; and 7, 8 & 9 for females.

Born in 1943 (癸未 guiwei), 59-year-olds:

People born in 1943, especially merchants, may have many chances, and are bound for achievement. Local and distant businesses, as well as work associates, may advance significantly, and if there are sufficient resources in manpower and

material, development can be expected. On the other hand, they should be wary of mean-spirited people who may ruin important projects.

Auspicious Numbers: 0 & 7 for males; and 0 & 7 for females.

Born in 1955 (乙未 *yiwei*), 47-year-olds:

Those born in 1955 have relatively good luck among all the people born in the Ram year. They have moderately good luck in making money, and they should remember that the best policy is to return on the gains and kindness they have received. Married people should take care in making friends of the opposite sex, and they should be restrained and well measured in speech and action.

Auspicious Numbers: 1 & 2 for males; and 2 & 9 for females.

Born in 1967 (丁未 *dingwei*), 35-year-olds:

Those born in 1967 are rather complacent this year. Things will go much more smoothly than last year, and they will have good opportunities in everything they do. Nevertheless, when they are enormously proud of themselves and ready for greater success, they should also be considerate to their kinsmen.

Auspicious Numbers: 4 & 7 for males; and 4 & 7 for females.

Born in 1979 (己未 jiwei), 23-year-olds:

Those born in 1979 can lay a solid foundation this year for their future career. If they can take the initiative, there will surely be a great development in their career. And they should pay attention to interpersonal relations, and guard against the hostility of others and the gossip that occurs behind their backs. Moreover they have extremely abundant emotions this year, so they have to take great cautions against undue love affairs to avoid mishaps.

Auspicious Numbers: 1, 6 & 9 for males; and 1 & 6 for females.

Born in 1991 (辛未 xinwei), 11-year-olds:

Children born in 1991 are better in health and schoolwork than last year, but they are still a bit distracted in their studies. It is better to give them a helping hand to achieve even better school records.

Auspicious Numbers: 8 & 9 for males; and 8 & 9 for females.

MONKEY

Prospects for those born in the Year of the Monkey

1908, 1920, 1932, 1944, 1956, 1968, 1980, 1992

People born in the Year of the Monkey have two auspicious stars this year: Taiying (太陰) (Moon) and Suihe (歲合)(Yearly Harmony). With the moon in mid-sky, night is shone nice bright. But there is a tendency of the male principle waning and the female principle waxing. And at the same time, there are four inauspicious stars shining: Guchen (孤辰)(Lonely Star), Guansuo(貫索) (Linked Chain), Goushen (勾神) (Soul Distracter) and Sanxing (三刑)(Three Tortures). Therefore, those born in the Year of the Monkey, especially males, may turn mishaps into good fortunes and have a plain sailing year so long as they faithfully

carry out their duties, behave discreetly and observe the law with auspicious stars coming to their rescue. This is testified in an old saying: Lead an honest and clean life with stability as the fortune; disaster may turn into good fortune, and guard against bloodshed. Although this is a capricious year with undercurrents lurking, there will be no serious problems this year so long as they make solid progress step by step, and take actions only after careful consideration.

Those born in the Monkey year have their prospects intermingled with both ill and good lucks, for this reason changes of a rather complicated nature will take place.

Males may have a possible work transfer, and it is easy for them to act and behave too rashly so as to invite defeat. Actually, a quiet observation is better than a reckless action. A good policy is to further improve themselves and continue to carry out their duties.

Females may have whimsical ideas about some trifles and they may even suffer frustrations because of materialism and foolery. So they should stick to their post and work in a down-to-earth way.

In terms of career, it will be a year that involves strenuous work, and it is not easy to succeed if they try to change their work. Some disputes may occur with seniors and superiors. So they should act carefully and properly to their status in dealing with everything.

As far as their luck in making money is concerned, they may not earn income as they wish and businessmen may have difficulties with fund circulation. Too much desire may invite mishaps.

In matters of love, lovers acquainted for longer periods may have success in marriage, yet hindrances might befall on newly acquainted partners. So they must take good care.

In family life, self-centeredness may lead to frictions between husband and wife, and disputes among family members. Consequently, consideration and tolerance are necessary to protect the family.

Regarding health, engorgement may cause stomach trouble. They should also pay due attention to eye and heart diseases, and make sure to get sufficient rest. They should also guard against unexpected traffic accidents.

Those born in the Year of the Monkey are sharp and intelligent, insightful and good at schemes. They are good at business management, and capable of getting an accurate grasp of the market and catering to the consumers' psychology with excellent results. They are confident, amusing and humorous, eloquent and good at expressing themselves. They are also full of energy and good at understanding other people's wishes.

Females born in the Year of the Monkey are bold and unrestrained and liberal in character, having a candid and natural charm. They will bring laughter

wherever they go, and males will be very much impressed. However, their vigor, vitality and flamboyant grace can also make males feel ashamed of themselves. And consequently, some males would rather make friends with females born in the Monkey year than marry them.

When well matched in marriage, people born in the Year of the Monkey will have a lovely and jolly family, enjoying a happy and perfectly satisfactory life with mutual understanding and accommodation.

Those born in the Monkey year will have SUPER LUCK when matched in marriage with those born in the years of the Rat and Dragon; they will have LUCK if matched in marriage with those born in the years of the Ox, Rabbit, Snake, Horse, Ram, Monkey, Rooster and Dog; they will have HALF ILL LUCK when they marry those born in the Year of the Pig; and they will have ILL LUCK when they marry those born in the Year of the Tiger.

The prospects of marriage for those born in the Year of the Monkey:

Auspicious: a perfect pair with plain sailing and no mishaps; enjoying riches, honor and success; descendents' continuous prosperity for five generations.

Inauspicious: misfortunes coming one after another at the beginning; fortunes expected in the old age; the middle aged having experienced one mishap after another; having no parents or other support; plagued by diseases; unduly death.

General prospects for those born in the Year of the Monkey

Born in 1920 (庚申 gengshen), 82-year-olds:

The elderly people born in 1920 should be taken good care of. Early treatments of many ailments may bring easy cures. They should be very careful when going up and down stairs, and reduce the number of times they move about.

Auspicious Numbers: 6 & 8 for males; and 6 & 7 for females.

Born in 1932 (壬申 renshen), 70-year-olds:

The elders born in 1932 should be more tolerant and try to get along with family members. They should try to be more open minded when frustrated and should avoid getting angry, and they should not vent, or shift their resentment to their spouses. In addition, they should guard against heart trouble.

Auspicious Numbers: 8 & 9 for males; and 7 & 8 for females.

Born in 1944 (甲申 jiashen), 58-year-olds:

People born in 1944 will not be very successful in doing things this year, and their work income will not be so ideal. They should properly abide by the law, observing cautiously instead of taking rash actions. Moreover, they should also guard against the destruction of fame and reputation for helping

their kinsmen. This is not a matter of losing money but the trouble of being involved in a lawsuit with officials. And finally they should guard against the harm done to their health through fatigue.

Auspicious Numbers: 0 & 8 for males; and 0 & 7 for females.

Born in 1956 (丙申 *bingshen*), 46-year-olds:

Those born in 1956 have a mixture of fortunes and mishaps. In the first half of the year, there will be some significant breakthroughs, but in the second half there might be quite a lot of hindrances. So they should take this opportunity and go all out, and make some efforts to put aside savings for something unexpected.

Auspicious Numbers: 2, 8 & 9 for males; and 2 & 9 for females.

Born in 1968 (戊申 *wushen*), 34-year-olds:

Those born in 1968 must keep a very sharp eye on people to ensure they aren't cheated out of their money. Businessmen engaged in manufacturing should guard against unexpected accidents. And their marriage or relationship might suffer a dissension caused by ill characters. It is advised to stay away from the red-light districts so as not to catch venereal diseases.

Auspicious Numbers: 4, 7 & 8 for males; and 4, 8 & 9 for females.

Born in 1980 (庚申 gengshen), 22-year-olds:

Those born in 1980 will not work or study with great facility this year, yet if they are not too quirky in thinking, they will do fine. Usually they must be cautious in speech and conduct to avoid trouble. There might be quite a few anecdotes involving feelings and emotions, but too much indulgence in love affairs may affect their career, and it may have some negative effects on those who enter a higher school.

Auspicious Numbers: 6 & 8 for males; and 6 & 9 for females.

Born in 1992 (壬申 renshen), 10-year-olds:

Children born in 1992 will make greater progress in their studies than last year, and they are in good health. They must, however, pay attention to safety when they take part in activities involving water. Just keep in mind the old saying: Braving the mountains rather than the waters.

Auspicious Numbers: 1, 8 & 9 for males; and 8 & 9 for females.

ROOSTER

*Prospects for those born
in the Year of the Rooster*

1909, 1921, 1933, 1945, 1957, 1969, 1981, 1993

People born in the Year of the Rooster have four auspicious stars: Sanhe (三合)(Three Harmonies), Jiangxing (將星) (General Star), Dijie (地解) (Earth Solution) and Luxun (祿勛)(Positional Merits) shining above with smooth prospects ahead. Yet, there are also four inauspicious stars coming along: Wugui (五鬼) (Five Devils), Guanfu (官符) (Official Insignia), Disha (地煞) (Sure Killer) and Nianfu (年符)(Yearly Incantation). Nevertheless, if they seek harmony and stability and progress step by step with great care, and with auspicious stars coming to their rescue, they may suffer no loss and turn mishaps into fortunes. Auspicious stars that shine high above

promise a bright perspective; and they should be cautious in speech and guard against robbery when going about. On the whole this will be a year of plain sailing. Though there may be some obstacles, sensible thinking may bring about quite good achievements.

Those born in the Rooster year have lucky stars shining overhead in their career prospects; either businessmen or employees may have smooth development. Even if there is some resistance in their way, it can be readily overcome. But they should keep in mind that they should not act on impulse and should not bite more than they can chew.

Financially, they may come across twists and turns. They should avoid speculation or gambling, otherwise they may suffer tragic losses.

In their career, they will have great achievements so long as they take the initiative and broaden their sphere of business. However, they must be aware that interpersonal troubles may impede them from going all out in their work.

In terms of their luck in making money, there is an unstable trend with undercurrents surging ahead this year. They should be cautious in financing, and save what they can for unexpected needs.

In matters of love they tend to have too strong an anxiety, so they have to guard against the possible destruction brought forward by the flaming sexual

desire which may do harm to others as well as themselves. They should be tender and considerate towards their spouses; they should be self-reliant and exercise good self-control to avoid the perpetual sorrow caused by an impulsive mistake.

In family life, husband and wife should take care not to get into undue disputes that may lead to serious conflicts just because of some trifles.

Regarding health, they should not neglect necessary rest. There might be troubles brought about by oral diseases. Yet there should be no great problems if they pay attention to their diet and daily life.

People born in the Year of the Rooster are smart and capable, full of energy and have a sense of justice. They are decisive and precise in their work. They have a quality of insight and premonition and are good at performance.

Those born in the Rooster year have an ardent love for beauty, and are naturally endowed with sensitivity for colors. They pay attention to their appearance and clothing with a graceful look and outstanding charm.

Females born in the Year of the Rooster will show their unusual qualities in ordinary circumstances. They are good at setting a nice balance between career and family, so they win high praises from males.

When well matched in marriage, people born in the Rooster year may lead a happy and satisfactory life with a successful career and a pleasant family.

Those born in the Year of the Rooster will have SUPER LUCK when matched in marriage with those born in the years of the Ox, Dragon and Snake; they will have LUCK if matched in marriage with those born in the years of the Tiger, Horse, Ram, Monkey and Pig; they will have HALF ILL LUCK when they marry those born in the years of the Rat, Rooster and Dog; and they will have ILL LUCK when they marry those born in the Year of the Rabbit.

The prospects of marriage for those born in the Year of the Rooster:

Auspicious: an everlasting fortune endowed by nature with both virtue and reputation accompanied by distinction, profits and honor; the highest respects and a very prosperous family.

Inauspicious: fiery and forthright in temper, but there may be some unpredictable mishaps; on no good terms between family members and hardly any male descendants; accompanied by various misfortunes; no great disasters, though.

General prospects for those born in the Year of the Rooster

Born in 1909 (己酉 *jiyou), 93-year-olds:*

The elderly people born in 1909 should reduce the number of times they move about and guard against injuries caused by falls. And ailments should get timely treatment.

Auspicious Numbers: 6 & 7 for males; and 1, 6 & 8 for females.

Born in 1921 (辛酉 *xinyou), 81-year-olds:*

The elderly people born in 1921 should be broad-minded, and rid themselves of fanciful ideas. They should take care when moving about to avoid limb injuries.

Auspicious Numbers: 7 & 8 for males; and 1, 8 & 9 for females.

Born in 1933 (癸酉 *guiyou), 69-year-olds:*

Those born in 1933 have rather good prospects, and live a leisurely life. To avoid bronchitis, they must pay attention to the changes in weather. They will enjoy a peaceful and happy life this year.

Auspicious Numbers: 8 & 10 for males; and 4, 7 & 10 for females.

Born in 1945 (乙酉 yiyou), 57-year-olds:

People born in 1945 have steady prospects this year. With many years of perseverance, their power may rise to a higher position. They may also have filial goodness and love. However, they must be careful in speech and manners with their spouses to prevent fierce conflicts.

Auspicious Numbers: 2, 4 & 7 for males; and 2 & 8 for females.

Born in 1957 (丁酉 dingyou), 45-year-olds:

Those born in 1959, either businessmen or employees, may have a very nice year. The outlook is very smooth with a huge amount of resources and wealth coming in. The pity is that there is a lack of manpower with very few capable associates, so they have to attend everything in person. Consequently, they should do things according to their abilities, and avoid any rash expansion. They should also take care of their health lest they should suffer a loss of money because of that.

Auspicious Numbers: 4, 7 & 9 for males; and 1, 4 & 8 for females.

Born in 1969 (己酉 jiyou), 33-year-olds:

People born in 1969 have good opportunities and luck financially, but they should never lay their hands on speculation or things associated with

gambling or lottery. Relationships and feelings should be dealt with properly, or they will become issues on which their spouses vent. They should also be on guard against sexual traps that may put them into everlasting sorrow caused by an impulsive mistake.

Auspicious Numbers: 6 & 7 for males; and 1, 6 & 7 for females.

Born in 1981 (辛酉 *xinyou), 21-year-olds:*

Those born in 1981 have very excellent perception, and for this reason, if they are not distracted, there will be some breakthrough in their studies. They should take care not to overdraw on their credit cards to avoid mishaps that will put them into deep debt and great trouble. They should also be on guard against ill characters. On the whole this will be a plain sailing year.

Auspicious Numbers: 1, 8 & 9 for males; and 8 & 9 for females.

Born in 1993 (癸酉 *guiyou), 9-year-olds:*

Children born in 1993 are clever and cute, and they will be better in health and studies than last year, but they are somewhat distracted in their studies. Their schoolwork can be further improved if they are given proper help.

Auspicious Numbers: 7 & 10 for males; and 8, 9 & 10 for females.

DOG

Prospects for those born in the Year of the Dog

1910, 1922, 1934, 1946, 1958, 1970, 1982, 1994

People born in the Year of the Dog have two auspicious stars: Yuede (月德)(Month Virtue) and Hongruan (紅鸞)(Red Phoenix). With Yuede shining above, mishaps may turn into fortune and both males and females will enjoy fame and honor; everything will be favorable. Yet at the same time there are four inauspicious stars in front: Sifu(死符)(Death Sign), Xiaohao (小耗)(Lesser Mouse), Yinsha (陰煞)(Moon Killer) and Ban'an (扳鞍)(Pull Saddle). However,

so long as they take precautions and are wary of backbites and slanders, and pay attention to good coordination, they will have help from sages, thus turning mishaps into fortunes and disasters into good luck. Everything will be safe and sound. Help from the sages facilitates a change for the better; they should pay attention to health and guard against quarrels and disputes. Generally, the prospect for this year is rather good. There might be some resistance, disputes or troubles, but careful conduct and hard work, with due attention to health, may help create a brand-new situation.

Those born in the Year of the Dog will have a plain sailing year and work will gradually development. The problems accumulated over the years will make a turn for the better, and they should persevere in their efforts. Yet there is a tendency that they may be ill prepared for the new plan, so they must be sensible in coping with the situation they find themselves in.

They may also get support from their superiors this year. It is better for them to cooperate with others; this may bring them fruitful results.

In terms of career, businessmen may have a flourishing development. If they can coordinate well with others, and make cautious advances in their work, it will be a very fortunate year. As for those employees, if they work in a down-to-earth way,

they will be very much appreciated.

Financially, there will be something for them to achieve, and they will not worry about daily expenses. There might be some good luck in speculation or gambling, but the operation should be kept well within their ability to handle.

In matters of love, it will be smooth going between people of different sexes, and the circles for association will be relatively wider than before.

In family life, there will be a harmonious atmosphere and few worries. But still they should have more communication with their family members.

Regarding health, though there will be few chances for diseases, they should take good care of their physique, and they should especially guard against heart or liver diseases.

People born in the Dog year are honest, but lacking in flexibility and tact. They are devoted and loyal to their career; they are active and energetic. They take love seriously and will be very careful in choosing a partner. They will treat their spouses very well after marriage, and they will be loyal to the family and take good care of children. They are popular with the females.

Females born in the Year of the Dog are lovely, pure and sensitive. They are ideal partners in the

minds of the males.

When well matched in marriage, those born in the Dog year will enjoy happiness in their relationship, and they will show mutual attachment and concern. They are good at children's education, so they will have a very harmonious and happy family.

Those born in the Year of the Dog will have SUPER LUCK when matched in marriage with those born in the years of the Tiger, Rabbit and Horse; they will have LUCK if matched in marriage with those born in the years of the Rat, Snake, Monkey, Dog and Pig; they will have HALF ILL LUCK when they marry those born in the years of the Ox, Ram and Rooster; and they will have ILL LUCK when they marry those born in the Year of the Dragon.

The prospects of marriage for those born in the Year of the Dog:

Auspicious: a good match endowed by nature that brings success to every undertaking; a good fortune in reverence and glory, in leisure and income; prospects of family prosperity and lasting luck and longevity.

Inauspicious: a match of wills with mishaps one after another; no big wealth, and hardly any good fortune or bright prospects; hardships and tribulations; nothing will be accomplished as wished.

General prospects for those born in the Year of the Dog

Born in 1910 (庚戌 gengshu), 92-year-olds:

The elderly people born in 1910 will have quite a few small troubles, so they must pay attention to ailments.

Auspicious Numbers: 1, 7 & 9 for males; and 1 & 7 for females.

Born in 1922 (壬戌 renshu), 80-year-olds:

The elderly born in 1922 are better in mood and health than last year. They should take care of their family dwellings, and get rid of fanciful ideas; then they may have a pleasant year.

Auspicious Numbers: 4 & 9 for males; and 1, 4 & 9 for females.

Born in 1934 (甲戌 jiashu), 68-year-olds:

Those born in 1934 are relatively poor in health, and they should pay attention to diet. They should not poke into other people's business, and they should guard against impulsive greed so that they are not taken advantage of by those who harbor ill intentions.

Auspicious Numbers: 1, 4 & 7 for males; and 1, 8 & 9 for females.

Born in 1946 (丙戌 bingshu), 56-year-olds:

Those born in 1946 will smoothly develop in their

career, but it is easy for them to be the target of gossip or rumors, so they must try to keep a low profile. Even if there are hurdles, they will be able to turn mishaps into fortune. However, they should not be too stubborn, and should remember to forgive others at the proper time.

Auspicious Numbers: 3, 8 & 9 for males; and 5 & 7 for females.

Born in 1958 (戊戌 *wushu*), 44-year-olds:

Those born in 1958 are not in a very good mood this year. They should strive for mutual understanding and concession to avoid a rupture in affection. And they should be cautious in making friends and guard against ill characters. In terms of work, they should try to take the initiative and pursue a change for the better in times of adversity. They should double their efforts and compensate for their deficiencies with diligence. They have good health themselves but there might be chances to attend funerals.

Auspicious Numbers: 5, 7, 8 & 9 for males; and 5 & 7 for females.

Born in 1970 (庚戌 *gengshu*), 32-year-olds:

Those born in 1970 may be swayed by emotional gains and losses this year, so they should try to be open-minded so their future is not impaired.

They should also heighten their awareness and guard against gossip and rumors. There may be no peace at home, so they must try to ease and reduce disputes. Generally, they are in good health. Occasional ailments will disappear with the use of medication.

Auspicious Numbers: 7 & 8 for males; and 1, 7, 8 & 9 for females.

Born in 1982 (壬戌 *renshu*), 20-year-olds:

Those born in 1982 have much better luck than last year, even if there may be difficulty with entering a higher school, or in employment and love. The problems may be settled soon. Family life will be rather pleasant and happy. The prospects will be very smooth.

Auspicious Numbers: 1 & 9 for males; and 1 & 9 for females.

Born in 1994 (甲戌 *jiashu*), 8-year-olds:

Children born in 1994 will be better in studies and health than last year, and they should be properly awarded and encouraged. Parents should remind them to make greater efforts, but they should be careful to not apply too much pressure on their children, lest things will go contrary to their wishes.

PIG

Prospects for those born in the Year of the Pig

1911, 1923, 1935, 1947, 1959, 1971, 1983, 1995

People born in the Year of the Pig have the auspicious star Yima (驛馬) (Post Horse) going in their way, which indicates gains in the far distance. They must travel afar and will enjoy splendid sights. However, they have four inauspicious stars coming along: Suipo(歲破) (Yearly Ruin), Dahao(大耗) (Great Depletion), Langan (欄干)(Blockage) and Pitou (披頭)(Disheveled Hair). They are prone to suffer the loss of money and wealth, and will be hurt by rumors. If they behave discreetly, and have an optimistic attitude while waiting for opportunities, they will be delivered out of disasters into good

84

fortune. In the year of Suipo, there will be a loss of wealth and bad luck with marriage. They should also guard against torture and injuries. They should have a positive attitude in such a situation, and be cautious in dealing with anything. They should treat friends and seniors well. Sages will come to their aid, thus turning mishaps into fortunes. There will be no serious problems.

Those born in the Pig year do not have a very plain sailing year because of the conflict between the Si (巳火) Fire and the Hai (亥水) Water. Yet if they try to carry out their duties faithfully without making any unpractical demands, they may have a peaceful time. However, if they over stretch their desire and demand, it is rather easy for them to suffer losses. This is something they should cautiously guard against.

Younger persons will be in an unstable mood, and if they react rashly, there will be no good results. So they should act sensibly.

The middle-aged are prone to suffer hindrances and misunderstandings, so they should be careful and cautious in the way they get along with other people.

The elderly people should faithfully carry out their own duties, and keep themselves in a pleasant mood.

In terms of career, even if they do their best, they can only maintain the status quo. New developments may result in disappointment. It is important to

manage time wisely at work to avoid being over tired. A change for the better can be expected.

Financially, it is easy for them to slip into luxury and extravagance. They should be moderate in their desires and practice saving for unexpected needs.

In matters of love, there may be some obstacles that prevent them from having a deeper mutual understanding of their partner. And at the same time, they should also be aware of temptations from the opposite sex.

Regarding health, they have no big problems. They should guard against headache and fever, paying special attention to a change in blood pressure and heart problems.

Those born in the Year of the Pig can work with endurance, and are good at trading. Owing to their honest and kind working style, they win good feelings from their work partners and investors, which allows them to have a very prosperous business. They are enterprising and broad-minded, with a determined will. They are characterized by optimism and chivalry, and they will take the initiative to help people of the opposite sex. They are tender and considerate, and are very popular with females.

Females born in the Pig year are thoughtful and good at understanding; they have genuine human interests, and are kind and tolerant, but naive. They are intelligent and will attach great importance to

feelings and are fond of grooming themselves. They are very faithful to love and are the real ladies in the minds of males.

When well matched in marriage, those born in the Pig year will have a happy and satisfactory family with both husband and wife faithful to love. They will attach great importance to family life.

Those born in the Year of the Dog will have SUPER LUCK when matched in marriage with those born in the years of the Rabbit and Ram; they will have LUCK if matched in marriage with those born in the years of the Rat, Ox, Tiger, Dragon, Horse, Rooster and Dog; they will have HALF ILL LUCK when they marry those born in the years of the Monkey and Pig; and they will have ILL LUCK when they marry those born in the Year of the Snake.

The prospects of marriage for those born in the Year of the Pig:

Auspicious: extremely prosperous for many generations; enjoying peace, respect and glory; a sure gain through charitable activities; happy celebrations for huge amounts of wealth; enjoying prosperity and descendents' success all their lives.

Inauspicious: hardly any harmony at home; suffering from loneliness and separation with little affection between family members; scarcely any great happiness all their life with an omen of untimely death.

General prospects for those born in the Year of the Pig

Born in 1923 (癸亥 guihai), 79-year-olds:

The elderly people born in 1923 will have to be looked after, and due attention should be paid to diabetes and heart trouble. They should be attentive to the safety of the family dwelling while keeping themselves in a good mood. They should try to be open-minded.

Auspicious Numbers: 0 & 8 for males; and 0 & 2 for females.

Born in 1935 (乙亥 yihai), 67-year-olds:

The elderly born in 1935 are in poor health, and it is easy for them to suffer injuries when falling. They should take good care and pay attention to the safety of the family dwelling, and be cautious when moving about. They should also be more lenient and tolerant towards others to help them avoid occasional depression.

Auspicious Numbers: 2 & 8 for males; and 1, 2 & 8 for females.

Born in 1947 (丁亥 dinghai), 55-year-olds:

Those born in 1947 have no serious problems in health, but they have to take care of their wives and children. They should remain cool and calm

in the face of rumors and gossip, and they also must look after their apprentices. If they carry out their duties properly, there will be satisfactory results.

Auspicious Numbers: 4 & 9 for males; and 4 & 9 for females.

Born in 1959 (己亥 jihai), 43-year-olds:

People born in 1959 have steady prospects. Their wives might suffer unexpected injuries, so they must be careful. They must make a calm analysis when going about things or making any decisions. It is best to make quiet observations rather than taking rash actions. Even though there might be some intangible resistance, satisfactory solutions will soon be found.

Auspicious Numbers: 6, 7 & 8 for males; and 1, 6 & 7 for females.

Born in 1971 (辛亥 xinhai), 31-year-olds:

Those born in 1971 may have quite a lot of disputes with friends, and this certainly will affect the relations and feelings for later days. Besides concessions, it is better to avoid contact and conflict. Both mental work and manual work are strenuous in their career, but no ideal return should be expected. Businessmen must be cautious with everything, as caution and care will help ensure a smooth and safe

journey forever forward.

Auspicious Numbers: 1, 8 & 9 for males; and 8 & 9 for females.

Born in 1983 (癸亥 *guihai*), 19-year-olds:

Those born in 1983 have a rather strong desire for knowledge this year, and they can get twice the result with half the effort in their studies. They will deal with their academic subjects and extracurricular activities with great ability. However, they should guard against distraction caused by love affairs lest they should botch their bright future.

Auspicious Numbers: 0, 2 & 6 for males; and 0, 2 & 7 for females.

Born in 1995 (乙亥 *yihai*), 7-year-olds:

Children born in 1995 are persistent in character, so they often will push their parents into rage. Parents should not curse or beat their children, and they should be patient in their instructions. This year it is easy for children to fall ill, so they should be taken good care of.

Auspicious Numbers: 2, 7 & 8 for males; and 2 & 6 for females.

II.

General Prospects
for the 12 Signs by month

RAT

Forecasts by month for those born
in the Year of the Rat
1912, 1924, 1936, 1948, 1960, 1972, 1984, 1996

-1st month *(Yin* 寅月, *Tiger's month)*
(February 4th to March 4th, 2001)

In order to guarantee the peace and safety of the New Year, those born in the Rat year should be cautious in everything they do. They should take care when having meals and guard against contagious diseases while hastily going about their business. There is some resistance in matters of love; you and your partner will experience different feelings and moods rather than the intrusion of a third person. The problem should be solved with patience and time. During this period, it is better to keep away from those places that provide unhealthy

entertainment to avoid rumors and gossip. There are troubles in their career as well, which requires clarification and effort to set things right, thus some kind of delay in work is inevitable. Nevertheless, they should be happy when the final results are satisfactory.

-2nd month (Mao 卯月, Rabbit's month)
(March 5th to April 4th, 2001)

The prospect for this month is rather obscure with so many obstacles in the way. They should not take any rash actions for the time being; it is better to wait for the right time. When going about outdoors, they must be extremely cautious lest there should be any unexpected accidents. The Northeast is the least appropriate direction in which to make any movements. When they have emotional fluctuations, they should try to get rid of impatience and irritation. Instead, they should be tender, accommodating and reconcilable so things do not get worse.

-3rd month (Chen 辰月, Dragon's month)
(April 5th to May 4th, 2001)

There is great improvement in prospects for this month. Difficult problems in their work and career can be settled in the second half of the month, and it can bring about financial gains. And there are chances to be recognized and appreciated by their superiors. They should have a good grasp of this opportunity and put forth their best efforts. There will be very good luck in making money; their regu-

lar income and side income are both rather bountiful. Nonetheless, troubles might come with money. In matters of love there may appear sunshine, warmth, liveliness and good feelings – the black clouds have changed to clear skies. Yet they should still stay away from sexual traps and debauchery to guard against future troubles.

-4th month (Si 巳月, Snake's month)
(May 5th to June 4th 2001)

The prospects for this month show a steady rising trend. The hindrances in career are gradually disappearing, which is a positive sign for change, expansion, new projects and opening up new markets. However, they may confront mean-spirited people this month, and they must guard against conflict generated by them. In terms of feelings, there might be a third person's intrusion that makes things complicated, but it is not proper to argue with them.

-5th month (Wu 午月, Horse's month)
(June 5th to July 6th, 2001)

There will be big expenses this month, and it is also possible to suffer the loss of money due to mistakes in planning. Care must be exercised when making investments; there is a sign for the loss of money. They must give very clear and thorough thought to business developments or work transfers. It will be favorable to cooperate with others in business. Things are smooth in matters of love; some small disagreements in opinion will not affect mutual feelings. They should be cautious when going

about things, and it is not proper to make any important decisions. In terms of family, there will be good luck with a decent family income. Please pay close attention to the safety of seniors' family dwelling.

- 6th month (Wei 未月, Ram's month)
(July 7th to August 6th, 2001)

The prospects for this month fall back; there is nothing special in work. They are diligent and thrifty with a steady luck in making money. Disputes and disagreements may occur, but they should not allow themselves to be too upset so they can live in peace with others. There might be a feeling of dullness in life, but their emotional life may be colorful. In terms of health, the prospects are not really strong. They should take good care of children's health.

-7th month (Shen 申月, Monkey's month)
(August 7th to September 6th, 2001)

This month promises very strong prospects with good development in their work. Rumors will disperse, and they will no longer be plagued with disputes. During this period, there will be very good luck in making money, and they may gain profit through investments. This month will bring them unusually good luck, though they may come across difficult problems. There will be great achievements in work, and they will obtain recognition and riches because they are wise, capable and powerful in handling problems.

-8th month *(You 酉月, Rooster's month)*
(September 7th to October 7th, 2001)

This month comes with wind, thunder and great waves that surge forward, so troubles and disputes will occur one after the other. They will be irritated, and even children will become their headache. However, they must cope with their problems with good composure, frankness and honesty. Yet the hurt feelings may disappear by themselves, and everything will be all right with a harmonious atmosphere at home. With solid relations and smooth love streaked with romance, their households are still out of the ordinary. In career and finance, the improvement in interpersonal relations may greatly facilitate their career advances. There may be some activities in investment and speculation, but they should not set too high an aim in their expectation. When going about outdoors, they should be careful to avoid unexpected accidents. They should be careful in doing everything.

-9th month *(Shu 戌月, Dog's month)*
(October 8th to November 6th, 2001)

The prospects for this month show strong motivation. In work they will have rich inspirations. If they can try hard to push their plan forward, there should be new breakthroughs. In addition there may come some new customers and clients. Young students will make great progress in their studies; their learning capability is much improved, and they will make progress in their studies. In terms of feelings and

love, they might make rash decisions or show a lack of tenderness because of their temporary irrational moods, which are not a result of real conflict.

-10th month (Hai 亥月, Pig's month)
(November 7th to December 6th, 2001)

The prospects for this month are turning for the better. There are some changes in the situation, so they are anxious to make some investments. They have many plans for their business, and they should carry out those plans if they are appropriate. They may make advances in their career during a stable situation, and there will be good results. Yet they should take heed to their speech, and remember the old saying: Mistakes often come from too much talking. It is beneficial to go out, and some love affairs may occur. In addition, the money left over should be put into savings. During this period, the most important thing is to take good care of their family members' health.

-11th month (Zi 子月, Rat's month)
(December 7th, 2001 to January 4th, 2002)

The prospects for this month are steady. There are hardships and obstacles in work, but difficulties and mishaps may be turned into good fortune. There may be some resistance in moving forward, yet their ambitions remain intact. They actively participate in all kinds of activities, busy with settling one problem after another, thus having some financial gains. However, it may also bring troubles so they must

be honest with their all customers, regardless of age, in their dealings. The busy month is also due to dinner parties and other social events. In terms of personal feelings, there may be some kind of neglect or fissure that leads to a complete rupture if it is not carefully nurtured.

-12th month (Chou 丑月, Ox's month)
(January 5th to February 3rd, 2002)
The prospects for this month are really favorable. Their luck in career may be rather smooth if work is done with facility, and finances are handled properly. However, there will also come some troubles. They may get bogged down with interpersonal problems, thus affecting their advances in work. For this reason, they must be on guard against troubles caused by improper remarks and avoid getting involved in disputes or conflicts. This will guarantee good achievements in this year's work. Regarding feelings and love, there will be good luck in general. Things will be romantic and warm, but they have to be on guard against the third person, which will be a challenge to their ability.

OX

*Forecasts by month for those born
in the Year of the Ox
1914, 1926, 1938, 1950, 1962, 1974, 1986, 1998*

-1st month (Yin 寅月, Tiger's month)
(February 4th to March 4th, 2001)

The problems of this year can be easily settled if those born in the Ox year can swallow their temporary anger during the New Spring. There will be quite a lot of twists and turns in career this month, and financially things will not be very good; it is not proper to make large investments. Entertainment around the New Year should be pursued within limits to avoid a tragic loss. During this period, they should try to be cautious about every-

thing rather than taking rash and hasty actions, otherwise it may be necessary to sacrifice their wealth to protect against disasters. Moreover, there might be misunderstanding in feelings or some hidden problems.

-2nd month (Mao 卯月, Rabbit's month)
(March 5th to April 4th, 2001)

This is a very favorable month with strong momentum and ascending prospects. They should not carry an arrogant air but instead they should be modest, which shows good upbringing and cultivation. They will have an income this month, but it comes through intense persuasion. A gain in fame and reputation is greater than a gain in wealth. There is a sign that shows the possession of great power for some time. There will also be some kind of cheating among friends, so it is necessary to be cautious. Matters of love will be like drinking nectar and having a visual feast, beautiful like the spring.

-3rd month (Chen 辰月, Dragon's month)
(April 5th to May 4th, 2001)

The prospects for this month show a gradual improvement, and financially luck will change for the better. Some external forces will come to their aid. In career they may improve a stagnant situation, but they may face fierce competition that requires them to apply great effort in their work. It is a good

time for going out. Unmarried persons when in love will have a nice time. Married persons should not neglect their partners to avoid a decline in their mutual affection.

-4th month (Si 巳月, Snake's month)
(May 5th to June 4th, 2001)

The prospects for this month are colorful, and wonderful luck in family life promises much happiness. Busy work brings good income accompanied by great advances in career. During this period, young people may have ideal results on examinations. They will be very popular among people in social circles. And old emotional troubles that have haunted them for quite some time will gradually disappear, and there is hope for a return to a relationship of the past.

-5th month (Wu 午月, Horse's month)
(June 5th to July 6th, 2001)

The prospects for this month go up steadily, with brightly shining promises. The interpersonal troubles pertaining to work have disappeared, and there will come help and support from good friends and relatives. They will no longer fight on their own. And in feelings there will be new chances. There will be significant improvement in their luck of making money, and investment may bring good profits, and moreover, unexpected gains may arrive as side income.

-6th month (Wei 未月, Ram's month)
(July 7th to August 6th, 2001)

The prospects for this month may be somewhat alternating with positive and negative elements; therefore career development may not come up as expected. They must be sensible when handling problems. Contracts should be laid out with great care in this month; there should be no negligence in signing anything. They should be familiar with all the details therein. It is absolutely necessary to think twice before making any decision so as to avoid any future troubles. Emotional problems will appear again. In a month that lacks the Moon, things will be obscure and vague. There will be a favorable turn, and it is still far away from the road to ruin. It is but a quick rain in the sunshine. Sunlight and overcast come in turns. There will be troubles all about, and casual talks may invite misfortunes.

-7th month (Shen 申月, Monkey's month)
(August 7th to September 6th, 2001)

They are not in a very good mood, feeling depressed and sick at heart. Such a mood will certainly affect the stability of their career. Hindrances in work will gradually disappear, without any unexpected twists. They should not be too stubborn in their opinions. As a matter of fact, this is not completely a month of bad luck. Financially there will be normal luck with usual income.

-8th month (You 酉月, Rooster's month)
(September 7th to October 7th, 2001)

In this month they will meet difficulties first, and then things will go in the direction of fortune and prosperity. There will be multiple sources for making money, so they should not be intimidated when difficulties arise. Their emotional state will become a laughing stock, and rumors, gossip and slanders will flood their lives. However, they have to make a firm decision about their intended partners, rather than being of two minds. They should also be on guard against diseases of the intestines and stomach, such as duodenal or stomach ulcers.

-9th month (Shu 戌月, Dog's month)
(October 8th to November 6th, 2001)

The prospects for this month fluctuate with auspicious or inauspicious elements interwoven. There are difficulties pertaining to their work, and there might be a gain in money through socializing and attending dinner parties. There will be no big problems, but they have to be on guard against getting cheated by others. Financially, there will not be good luck, so it is not proper to get involved in rash investments and gambling. They should be cautious in handling their finances, keeping a close watch for new investment opportunities. They should try banking, stocks and securities.

-10th month (Hai 亥月, Pig's month)
(November 7th to December 6th, 2001)

Perseverance and endurance are required for this month. Although many things are delayed, and luck seems capricious, they have to keep a high morale for there will be no lack of fighting spirits. There may be some conflict with customers or clients. In term of family life, the prospects are rather good. There will be a nice family income, and the investments for the family as a unit have shown good results, good income. Regarding feelings, there might be some disturbance, but they should never act on impulse, but make a rational and calm choice. It is not proper to develop an underground love affair. On the whole, this is a month in which many achievements will be made in spite of difficulties, and there will be profits and gains.

-11th month (Zi 子月, Rat's month)
(December 7th, 2001 to January 4th, 2002)

The prospects for this month present a brand-new look. Everything should be handled with great ease, and there may be significant achievements. During this period it is favorable to go on errands for business, and business talks will have good chances for success. However, they should guard against over excitement, so as not to fall in business traps caused by temporary neglect. And during this period they must be sharp enough to see through different types of people, in order to avoid getting blamed for mak-

ing bad friends. Therefore, they must do everything carefully, and special care must be given to their career development.

-12th month (Chou 丑月, Ox's month)
(January 5th to February 3rd, 2002)

The horoscope for the whole year is by no means bad. People born in the Year of the Ox are generally open-minded and in a good mood, fond of going about busy with work. So they should take care in doing everything. It is beneficial for them to leave home for business, yet they need to remember to budget time for themselves. This month, at the end of the year, promises no great gains, yet there is no big trouble either. They just have to pay close attention to health. There might be some undercurrents emotionally, which will cause stagnancy. They should be patient and tolerant. It may be financially viable for spouses to leave home to make money, but they are somewhat weak in constitution and should guard against bad health due to alcohol and sex.

TIGER

*Forecasts by month for those born
in the Year of the Tiger*
1914, 1926, 1938, 1950, 1962, 1974, 1986, 1998

-1st month (Yin 寅月, Tiger's month)
(February 4th to March 4th, 2001)

This is a period of poor prospects with many twists and turns in the work of those born in the Year of the Tiger. However there are opportunities for a change in their career, but it requires calm and composure rather than taking rash actions. There might be complicated emotional problems, but they should not play with the fire or they may burn themselves. They should pay due attention to social

gatherings and be careful with foods. They should understand that peace and security are good fortune. They should guard against injuries; they are prone to limb injuries. If there are any diseases, early treatments are absolutely necessary, and they should not hide their illness for fear of treatment.

-2nd month (Mao 卯月, Rabbit's month) (March 5th to April 4th, 2001)

There are lucky stars shining overhead this month. Great momentum will gradually gather its strength with the Sun rising to the zenith in the sky. In spite of hardships, there will be good income; there will be vast financial improvements. During this period, it is important to be aware of gossip. The schoolwork of children may be their headache. Since their lovers or spouses are very strict, they should try to avoid harm from sex and alcohol. There will be an improvement in health, but they should still be wary of the hygiene of foods and drinks.

-3rd month (Chen 辰月, Dragon's month) (April 5th to May 4th, 2001)

There will be achievements in their work, and they will win praises for their steady progress. They will also have good income. There will be quite a lot of social gatherings, and they run the danger of getting bogged down in recreational or entertaining places with extravagant atmospheres and the temptation of sex, alcohol and wealth. They should pay strict attention to the development of their work and guard against unexpected troubles, for a little negligence may cause big blunders in an otherwise favorable situation. There might be some fluctuations emotionally, and they should try to protect their relationships carefully, otherwise it might be too late for them to repent.

-4th month (Si 巳月, Snake's month) (May 5th to June 4th, 2001)

There is a sudden change in perspective; those born in the Tiger year may have unsteady prospects with many twists and turns. With luck in making money in an unfavorable status, there should not be any important investment, and they should never lay their hands on gambling. Because luck happens to be in a rather weak status financially, they should not expect too much from either regular income or side income. There are still many obstacles in the way of work development. They might be sent away to work in other places, or they may leave home in order to make money. Anyway they will be busy going about. For this reason, those born in the Year of the Tiger should be cautious in their work. They should work according to their abilities, and never over work lest they should break

down from stress. Emotionally they will be unpredictable. It is necessary to communicate more with their lovers to guard against rifts in feelings.

-5th month (Wu 午月, Horse's month)
(June 5th to July 6th, 2001)

Those born in the Year of the Tiger should take the good opportunity to make advances, for in this month they may have the blessings from the God of prosperity. The dark clouds overhead may be dispelled and a new perspective will present itself. In spite of the tough competition, the launching of new projects may help get twice the result with half the effort. However, there must be a lot of advance preparation, and only a good beginning can bring about good results in the end. They should guard against friction with their subordinates, and try to overcome interpersonal problems. They should take care not to get hurt by sharp-edged tools or dog bites. If their fathers are old and get sick, they should take extremely good care of them.

- 6th month (Wei 未月, Ram's month)
(July 7th to August 6th, 2001)

For this month, they must take care of everything themselves. They should not readily believe rumormongers. The most important is they should not depend upon others completely to avoid being

cheated or betrayed. And there are still many difficult problems waiting for them to handle. Their
ability to settle problems is marvelous, and this is a
good time for them to demonstrate their ability and
determination. They will be a strong leader at their
workplace because of this. However they should
not neglect their better half; they need not only
love and care but also romance and enjoyment.

-7th month (Shen 申月, Monkey's month)
(August 7th to September 6th, 2001)

In this month it is better for them to observe quietly rather than act recklessly. They must be prepared for danger in times of safety. The prospects
for this month seem to be calm and tranquil on the
surface, but there are undercurrents surging forward. If they do not sharpen their vigilance, they
might suffer a great loss in a seemingly favorable
situation. Their luck in making money will suffer
a disastrous decline, and there will also be traps
with lures of money. They need to take care not to
fall in by mistake. They are not very good in health,
and they should get rid of bad habits involving
smoking, alcohol and sex. In their career there are
many obstacles in the way. During this period they
must make plans for the future before taking action. It is absolutely not proper to travel afar and it

is better to cancel all their plans to leave home. If they have to go outdoors, they must be extremely careful and guard against unexpected accidents. Their lovers are at odds with them, and warm feelings are replaced by irritation and depression.

-8th month (You 酉月, Rooster's month) (September 7th to October 7th, 2001)

Luck in making money for this month is very good, and it is quite profitable to invest. This month promises a strong rise in prospects, as the Sun is shining at its zenith. Love is like taking a shower in the bright sunshine, and the dark clouds over the love matters of last month will be dispelled. Their relationship will be lukewarm for the time being, but so long as they persist in their efforts, the lovers will be enthusiastic again. Unfortunately, there is always some trouble, and they should be careful with people, even with their friends. The important thing is health; they should pay attention to stomach troubles and intestine discomfort. In addition, they should stay away from alcohol and sex traps.

-9th month (Shu 戌月, Dog's month)
(October 8th to November 6th, 2001)

There are disputes and disagreements at home, and extramarital love affairs. This month will be a real test. Each side claims to be correct, and there is a possibility of a big bawl that will push them into a bad mood. The relations with others are not very good, and disputes exist. When going out, they should be on guard against unexpected accidents. Their superiors are very nice to them, so work will be smooth and appreciation can be expected. The prospects for this month are steady, while they should not seek great success and contributions; they should try to avoid any mistakes or faults. Peace and stability are the most important at the present stage.

-10th month (Hai 亥月, Pig's month)
(November 7th to December 6th, 2001)

To be tolerant is the best policy for this month. The prospects for this month look rather bewildering. They should try to avoid trouble and lawsuits and try to guard against ill-spirited persons. Troubles may take place among friends, so they should refrain from talking too much to avoid mistakes. In terms of work they will have many challenges. Hindrances appear one after another, and success will only come after a long and anxious wait. With a strong rival in front, careful planing and decision must come before action. If this is not done, they will fail on the verge of success and chances are that others may gain the upper hand. During this period it is important to quietly observe the situation. Remember, hardships will turn into good fortune. The greater the difficulties, the greater the future achievements. There are also some problems regarding real estates as well as disturbances at home.

-11th month (Zi 子月, Rat's month)
(December 7th, 2001 to January 4th, 2002)

Some tough problems and delays in work may be solved this month. When they take a deep breath, they should be cautious not to be deceived. In this month, there are ill characters staging backbites, so they should heighten their watchfulness to avoid getting taken in. Moreover, they should not borrow any money. Troubles and misunderstanding will bring about bad moods. They really want to be decisive, yet the circumstance will not allow them to be. Unmarried people might attract partners. They are in good health and full of vitality, so it is all right to travel afar. But care should be taken to guard against unexpected mishaps.

-12th month (Chou丑月, Ox's month)
(January 5th to February 3rd, 2002)

People born in the Year of the Tiger have an ordinary perspective this year, and fortunately there will be good progress at the end of the year. If they can go on with their efforts, the end of the year will be splendidly bright, just as the bright Moon can be seen when the dark clouds disperse. Although there may be some tough questions, there will be sages coming to their help. They should have confidence in their work if they remember that more work brings more gains, and more efforts bring more fortune. Their spouses may have good luck in making money, and the house will be full of songs. They will turn to a new page emotionally that is rich and colorful. At the beginning of the month, they must pay very close attention to traffic safety.

RABBIT

*Forecasts by month for those born
in the Year of the Rabbit*

1915, 1927, 1939, 1951, 1963, 1975, 1987, 1999

-1st month (Yin 寅月, Tiger's month)
(February 4th to March 4th, 2001)

There are steady prospects in the New Spring
this year, and financial gains will be rather
smooth. In career there will be help from sages.
People born in the Year of the Rabbit should
follow the prescribed order in everything they
do, and they should not act with undue haste or
set too high a demand. And in this way they
will feel very lucky, and will be happy. In business there will be many new contacts and ties,

and rather successful as well. Luck in making money is quite good, and during this period there will be a small fortune to be made. In matters of love, there will be new developments, so they will be riding on the crest of success.

-2nd month (Mao 卯月, Rabbit's month)
(March 5th to April 4th, 2001)

It is required this month to have a very sharp mind. There will be some twists and turns in their work, with hard work bringing no gains at all. Yet they should be patient. Difficult problems in work will demand a show of their real ability and wisdom. And when the tough issues are settled, they will win even greater respect. Luck in making money is not so good, and it is not proper to be involved in gambling or new investments. And during this period, it is probable they will suffer unexpected injuries, and disasters may have to be shielded by the loss of wealth.

-3rd month (Chen 辰月, Dragon's month)
(April 5th to May 4th, 2001)

There is a slight improvement in prospects this month, but it seems success that is within reach is lost again. Although the way to excel at work is still rather haphazard, great advances have been made. In terms of health they should avoid

exhaustion, or in the coming two or three months they will be constantly plagued by diseases. And during this period they must be very careful financially to avoid stagnancy in the circulation of their funds. Feelings and love are developing steadily, and they should have their temper under good control; undisciplined behavior will do harm to feelings.

-4th month (Si 巳月, Snake's month)
(May 5th to June 4th, 2001)

The prospects for this month seem to be fluctuating; undesirable things will come one after another, so they should be mentally prepared in advance. There will be twists and turns in their career, but they should not stop half way because later this year there will be great achievements. They should guard against undue love affairs that may lead to a tragic loss of money.

-5th month (Wu 午月, Horse's month)
(June 5th to July 6th, 2001)

There is no great improvement in the prospects of this month. They cannot take any chances in work because there are still some unexpected difficulties, and even serious disputes. They must remain calm in handling these problems. They must have self-control because they are in high

spirits and there might be some change in behavior or manners. Therefore, they should have
a good check on themselves and do things cautiously. Overwork and fatigue might cause some
health problems, so they must take good care of
themselves. They should watch for fever and diseases associated with the head and eyes, as well
as heart and blood diseases. Otherwise they
might be hospitalized and require surgical operations.

-6th month (Wei 未月, Ram's month)
(July 7th to August 6th, 2001)

Out of the depth of misfortune comes bliss. The
prospects for this month are steadily going up.
Great successes are behind the tough problems,
and the final victory will belong to them. They
may find no way out at the beginning, but persistence will surely lead to solution. If they are
very cautious in finance, this month's income will
be very handsome. As far as feelings are concerned, there might be some problems. They
should give heed to problems with the stomach
and intestines.

-7th month (Shen 申月, Monkey's month)
(August 7th to September 6th, 2001)

The prospects for this month are still unrestricted. The advances in work are rather smooth, and luck with making money can still be good. However, during this period due attention must be paid to safety, and they should try to be on guard especially against dangers caused by water. No one can be too careful. There is good luck in the household with an increased income. However, nothing is clear in matters of feelings. It is still rather complicated and confusing.

-8th month (You 酉月, Rooster's month)
(September 7th to October 7th, 2001)

The prospects for this month will have an unfavorable turn, so luck may not be as good as before. They may be worried about numerous problems. There is still some kind of momentum in their career, and they cannot avoid bustling about. They are in relatively good health, but they should also take good care of old people at home, for parents may have the feeling of loneliness. The chances for attending funerals cannot be ruled out. In work there are also people who will highlight their faults and be extremely particular about their work. It is better to be tolerant for the time being.

-9th month (Shu 戌月, Dog's month)
(October 8th to November 6th, 2001)

The prospects for this year are quite volatile, but fortunately there are auspicious stars in the palace of destiny coming to help. If they can lay a solid foundation with unremitting efforts, the mishaps may turn into good fortune. Their perseverance in the last nine months will bring good achievements in the next three months of the year, and the joy brought therefrom may greatly enhance self-confidence. They will assume an air of big wheels by looking grand and perky among friends. There will be a lot of social interaction, so they should be fully aware of their workload. Luck in money making is good, with wealth coming their way. Yet when elated with fame and gain, they should never forget to stop within a proper boundary.

-10th month (Hai 亥月, Pig's month)
(November 7th to December 6th, 2001)

There is some resistance in terms of luck in making money at the beginning, but there will be help from sages. The prospects are average. In work they should be careful with something unexpected; they should not take rash actions. Moreover there might be some customers or clients writing to complain, and this should be

handled with great care. In this month, your superiors and seniors may have magnificent luck; either achievements or wealth will allow them to be shining in front of others. Their emotions are getting more and more complicated, so they should try to make an early and decisive choice.

-11th month (Zi 子月, Rat's month)
(December 7th, 2001 to January 4th, 2002)

The prospects for this month fall back a little, but those born in the Rabbit year are still busy with their work and advances are still appreciated. They will receive praise from their superiors, and enjoy a good reputation. Unfortunately they might be weak in energy and not be very well in health, so they must take good care of themselves. During this period, they must stay away from debauchery, so as to prevent their health from worsening. Luck for extra income shows a sign of decline, so they should not be too anxious about extra income. They might have verbal misunderstandings with their spouses or sweethearts. There might be disputes or quarrels with friends, and they should remember that too much talk will lead to blunders.

-12th month (Chou丑月, Ox's month)
(January 5th to February 3rd, 2002)

A year of hard work is bringing about good results at the end of the year, so they are extremely busy with work, bustling about with no chance for a rest. However, the busier they are, the happier they seem to be. At this time they are sharp-minded, good at planning, and good at settling tough problems. There will come new opportunities, and they should have a firm grasp of the occasion. Regarding feelings there appears to be a favorable turn; they will take great pleasure in a sweet and cozy love. It is advised to go out and enjoy a two-person world.

DRAGON

*Forecasts by month for those born
in the Year of the Dragon*

1916, 1928, 1940, 1952, 1964, 1976, 1988, 2000

*-1st month (Yin 寅月, Tiger's month)
(February 4th to March 4th, 2001)*

In the spring of this New Year there are auspicious stars shining high, so there is power and momentum shown in the career of those born in the Dragon year. They are full of vigor and vitality and are working with facility. But the gain is overshadowed by fame. Money will come and go with a two-to-one proportion for gains and losses, i.e. two items of income versus one item

of expense; entertainment, banquets and so on will naturally increase expenditure. And during this period there will be a new emotional breakthrough: warm and harmonious, elated and happy.

-2nd month (Mao 卯月, Rabbit's month)
(March 5th to April 4th, 2001)

The prospects for this month seem rather fluctuating and paradoxical, and this is especially true of luck in money making during the first half of the month. It is not necessary to be oversensitive, but they have to guard against mistakes or deception in the investments of foreign currencies or stocks and securities. Unmarried persons may be acquainted with new partners, but they should not be beside themselves with extreme joy.

-3rd month (Chen 辰月, Dragon's month)
(April 5th to May 4th, 2001)

In this month there is a sudden change in the situation, so they should not try to cut a smart figure but instead they should keep a low profile. It is always harmful to show off and attempt something impossible, and there are already many hindrances in the advancement of work with unexpected incidents. They should keep in mind that impulsive emotions should never cause disputes. They should be careful with everything. There are ups and downs in luck with making money, so they should give up unreasonable demands. Moreover, they should pay attention to foods and drinks to keep fit. Feelings are experiencing fluctuations; sometimes they will be in good moods and sometimes in bad. They should try to avoid troubles thus improving the harmony in feelings and relations.

-4th month (Si 巳月, Snake's month)
(May 5th to June 4th, 2001)

The prospects for this month are rather smooth and gratifying, and in career there will be great advances. They must understand that there are various chances, and they should not delay in action. Luck in making money is changing for the better with a sign of good side income. Sometimes there will be unexpected gains. During this period there will be good results on exams. There will be problems in matters of feelings and love. It will be a hard time for husbands and male friends. They will feel rather lonely. They should guard against rivals of the opposite sex.

-5th month (Wu 午月, Horse's month)
(June 5th to July 6th, 2001)

According to the prospects of this month, it is better to take action rather than to observe quietly. There is some stagnancy in work and quite a lot of gossip and rumors, too. It is an unfavorable month for males; and for this reason, males must be extremely cautious when going outside. But the focus of attention should be put on finances, for there is the possibility of suffering a loss in money. They should especially guard against their money and wealth getting robbed by others. In the aspects of feelings, the perspective is rather obscure. They are not in a good mood, and quarrels and disputes may take place from time to time. In this case, they should be tolerant.

-6th month (Wei 未月, Ram's month)
(July 7th to August 6th, 2001)

Some kinds of changes are still in progress, and development in other places shows a steady situation. On the whole, prospects are gradually entering a good status. The financial crisis is disappearing, but it is still necessary to be cautious with investments. Their love and emotions have become steady again. And so long as they understand romance, there will be great happiness be-

tween those of the opposite sex. Lovers may have very rich and colorful times together. They should not be afraid of any discord in feelings, yet they may come across some sudden resistance.

-7th month (Shen 申月, Monkey's month)
(August 7th to September 6th, 2001)

The prospects for this month are smooth and fluent; they feel good in body and mind. Sages may also come and help. If they work hard in an unremitting way, there will be lots of sources for making money. They will be very busy, and at this time the busier they are, the more profits they may obtain. However, they are somewhat lonely at heart. On the whole, they should have a clear objective in view, and set a clear separation between friends and lovers to avoid misunderstanding or getting entangled in love affairs, which will mar their future.

-8th month (You 酉月, Rooster's month)
(September 7th to October 7th, 2001)

Prospects this month are auspicious. Those born in the Dragon year will be sound in body and mind. As far as work is concerned, it is proper to seek wealth away from home, thus gaining profits in other places. Sages will also help. Their

regular income is very steady, yet to seek side income is not proper at the moment. There are hindrances in work, but fortunately all the problems can be readily solved. They should never allow their elation to get the best of them. They should pay attention to foods and drinks and get proper rest, for over fatigue will cause diseases of the stomach and digestive system. There will be some love affairs outside, and they will be very popular with persons of the opposite sex. It is likely that they will be a smart figure socially.

-9th month (Shu 戌月, Dog's month) (October 8th to November 6th, 2001)

There is a sudden change in the prospects for this month; there will be crises, resistance, failure in carrying out plans and other interruptions in career. They will better cope with this ever-changing situation with calm observation. They should remember that hardships will turn into good fortune, and the difficulties will surely be overcome, it is only a matter of time. For this reason, it is not proper to make big investments, and there will be great pressure in work. During this period, they should pay attention to feelings, for there will be many twists and turns. But for the time being, taking no measure is bet-

ter than taking any measure, because any efforts will be spent in vain.

-10th month (Hai 亥月, Pig's month)
(November 7th to December 6th, 2001)

After the hard struggle of last month, the prospects for this month are mingled with auspicious and sinister elements, but at last there comes a newly opened situation. Therefore, they should heighten their vigilance, and make solid advances rather than taking rash actions. And if they are not careful financially, they may find themselves in an economic plight. There will be no great problems in health, but the pity is that there will be failures in matter of feelings. Patient explanation will not help solve problems and the more they talk, the more mistakes they might make, causing more misunderstanding.

-11th month (Zi 子月, Rat's month)
(December 7th, 2001 to January 4th, 2002)

Luck in money making will improve greatly this month, as if the sun is shining at its zenith. There will be great gains in both reputation and profits. There will also be great advances in work. Both regular income and side income are quite

promising, but there are still some undercurrents. They will not be very healthy, and care must be taken to protect their liver and kidneys. Their sadness emotionally is not due to a third person. There is no impulse of love, but a feeling of obscurity and vague melancholy.

-12th month (Chou 丑月, Ox's month) (January 5th to February 3rd, 2002)

The prospects tend to be steady. There will be great achievements in work and financially they will earn a handsome income. Luck is wonderful both in career and in finance. In terms of feelings, both sides are rather subjective, stubborn and tenacious, and are not willing to give in. But during this period there will be chances for them to be reconciled thus mending their old relations.

SNAKE

*Forecasts by month for those born
in the Year of the Snake*

1916, 1928, 1940, 1952, 1964, 1976, 1988, 2000

*-1st month (Yin 寅月, Tiger's month)
(February 4th to March 4th, 2001)*

During the spring of the New Year there is something inauspicious, so there are many obstacles. The career has been rather smooth, but there always come some delays without rhyme or reason. It is necessary to take preventive measures

as early as possible, so as to avoid awkward situations where urgent missions cannot wait for preparation. It is most necessary during this period to achieve solidarity and pool the wisdom and efforts of everyone. They should go all out to avoid a loss in business. They should not leave any chance for the opponents to defeat them. It is not favorable to leave home, and they should guard against injuries. They are not very good in health, so they should pay close attention to diseases related to their liver and kidneys.

-2nd month (Mao 卯月, Rabbit's month) (March 5th to April 4th, 2001)

Ordinary and insipid are the characteristics of the prospects for this month. Some people have side income. Luck in making money is rather good, it is favorable to earn side income, and so playing with small stakes will bring some results They should not take rash actions, but instead, they should think twice before taking any action. There will be a lot of social functions with wines, wealth and money, and it is rather easy to encounter irrational love affairs. The prospects for work are steady, while their romantic relationship will suffer from quarrels and a temporary separation.

-3rd month (Chen 辰月, Dragon's month)
(April 5th to May 4th, 2001)

The prospects for this month are rather zigzag-ging, but they may gradually enter a favorable phase. Financially they have rather good luck, though at the beginning of the month there will be some difficulties or stagnancy, so it is not proper to gamble or to invest. The gains will finally arrive when the difficulties are overcome. Luck in money making will have a change for the better at the middle of the month. In terms of work there will be new ideas or conceptions, and new breakthroughs. The relations between husband and wife and between lovers still make them disconsolate. The relations are peaceful and harmonious on the surface, yet there are under-currents lurking. When dealing with other people or traveling away from home, they should be on guard against troubles caused by casual remarks; they should be cautious in coping with the situation.

-4th month (Si 巳月, Snake's month)
(May 5th to June 4th, 2001)

The prospects for this month are fluent and flamboyant. There will be greater pressure in their work, so they have to become absorbed in their work and give it their all. They should value good opportunities, and even if there are frustrations they should not give up. The problems can be readily solved. During this period, they must try to take the initiative. They should also guard against ill-spirited people trying to rob them of their achievements. They should also try to avoid offending their superiors. Care must be taken to guard against some hidden diseases.

-5th month (Wu 午月, Horse's month)
(June 5th to July 6th, 2001)

The prospects for this month are rather strong. They have very good fortune in monetary matters because lucky stars shine for money making. In work, they are also very popular with colleagues, and they can make good use of their relations with these people. They should take the opportunity to move ahead and obtain excellent results, thus greatly facilitating their career development. There may also be members of the

opposite sex around, but they should not be beside themselves to avoid falling into sex traps. Their family life is stable, and they have good relations with their seniors and superiors.

-6th month (Wei 未月, Ram's month)
(July 7th to August 6th, 2001)

The prospects for this month are so brilliant. In career, they will have the upper hand over their rivals, winning important customers and contracts. Financially, there is still a good perspective that promises a wonderful return. It is proper to make important investments. There is great improvement in health, and they are no longer plagued by disease. Luck in romance appears rather vague and fuzzy, so they should never be careless about it.

-7th month (Shen 申月, Monkey's month)
(August 7th to September 6th, 2001)

In this month, there will be dark clouds overhead and undercurrents lurking, therefore it is better to take the defensive position rather than the offense in business. They should guard against the possibility of being taken advantage of at a weak point. They should not get over fatigued in order to avoid getting stressed out

or catching some hidden diseases. There is some tension between husband and wife and between lovers. So there will be no peace at home, only quarrels and disputes.

-8th month *(You 酉月, Rooster's month)*
(September 7th to October 7th, 2001)

There are signs for improvement in prospects this month, but the trend seems to be full of twists and turns. Though there are no big problems in business, there are still some small difficult points. They are in very good shape to cope with these problems, thus winning due respects. In the second half of the month, they have two items of income coming through two channels. There are sages coming to help in their work, and lovers are very enthusiastic. However, during this period they must try to get more rest, because they may fall victim to headaches and insomnia.

-9th month (Shu 戌月, Dog's month)
(October 8th to November 6th, 2001)

The prospects for this month are quite smooth and flamboyant, which indicates there will be great achievements in career because things will be handled with facility and auspicious stars will come to help. They should bring their real ability into play, but they should guard against ill characters at their work. They will be caught unprepared with troubles all about if they are not careful. The more explanation, the worse the situation will be. Luck in making money is rather good, but they should not be too greedy about side income. If they could stop within limits, there may be unexpected joy. There may be some quarrels between spouses and between lovers over some trifles. The best policy will be tolerance.

-10th month (Hai 亥月, Pig's month)
(November 7th to December 6th, 2001)

In this month, there are inauspicious stars gathering overhead. For this reason, the prospects have a sudden change for the worse, full of danger and perils. They may try all they can to solve problems at work, but the situation may still worsen, wasting their previous efforts. Arguments will become disputes and quarrels, and

their superiors may get involved in troubles and lawsuits. During this period, close attentions should be paid to their health to keep away disease.

-11th month (Zi 子月, Rat's month)
(December 7th, 2001 to January 4th, 2002)

The prospects for this month make a turn for the better, gradually entering a favorable phase. The obstacles in work are gradually dispelled and there may come a breakthrough in development. Too much talk will often bring about mistakes, so they should be extremely cautious when they speak at meetings. They have good luck in making money, so they can make investments with ease. There is improvement in health with each passing day, but they still should take good care. While traveling around, there will be romantic anecdotes, but it is difficult to tell whether it is a blessing or a mishap, so they should be careful.

In career, the auspicious and inauspicious elements are mixed up this month; they should be very cautious in their work. The luck in making money is fluctuating, so they should not make too high a demand. They should, on the other hand, pay close attention to the safety of family habitation and prevent elderly people and young children from falling and getting injured. In addition they should be on guard against disasters pertaining to bloodshed. There is discord between lovers and between husband and wife. If they are to get married at the end of the year, they have to be careful. They should be prepared for unexpected accidents.

HORSE

*Forecasts by month for those born
in the Year of the Horse*

1906, 1918, 1930, 1942, 1954, 1966, 1978, 1990

*-1st month (Yin 寅月, Tiger's month)
(February 4th to March 4th, 2001)*

There is good luck in the New Spring. There
will be trouble when their career begins, but
great advances will follow. At the moment fame
is greater than gain. Luck in money making is
normal, with a good chance of increasing
wealth. Good results may be expected because

they have a very strong desire to make investments and take action. There will be a lot of social gatherings with banquets and beauties, wealth and jewelry. They will be rather popular with people of the opposite sex. Spouses and lovers show sweet tenderness and attachment. Regarding health, they should avoid alcohol and sex, and go on a diet.

-2nd month (Mao 卯月, Rabbit's month) (March 5th to April 4th, 2001)

The prospects for this month are fluctuating. As far as career is concerned, there are dark clouds overhead, and there often occur unexpected new problems. There must be careful planning for countermeasures. During this month there will be quite a lot of fair-weather friends and the schoolwork of the young people may not come up to their expectation; they must make painstaking efforts. In addition, they must understand that they should not cram for examinations. In matters of love, there is no sign of a change for the better.

-3rd month (Chen 辰月, Dragon's month)
(April 5th to May 4th, 2001)

The prospects for this month are fluctuating, and luck in making money is not very good. They should be very cautious with their investments, and it is not proper to get involved in speculative dealings. Then there will be normal luck in money making. Attempts to earn a side income or gambling are far from appropriate. In their work they should be on guard against some people striving to drive a wedge between them and their bosses or superiors. Regarding health, they should be careful with symptoms related with the heart, lungs and blood pressure, and there should be no negligence. As for spouses or lovers, they should let fate take its own course and avoid unnecessary friction.

-4th month (Si 巳月, Snake's month)
(May 5th to June 4th, 2001)

The prospects for this month are superbly favorable; they will be joyful and jubilant. Especially in terms of feelings, their life is rich and colorful. It is favorable to leave home, and the Northeast is the best direction. There might be an interesting anecdote during the journey. It is proper to make investments this month. They are likely to get profits through solid and steady

policy and business. It will be favorable to invest in stocks and securities. People of the opposite sex will constantly appear, but they must understand how to make a wise choice.

-5th month (Wu 午月, Horse's month)
(June 5th to July 6th, 2001)

This month they will encounter a very difficult problem at the beginning. Developments at work are quite mediocre and there is no good luck in money making, so it is not proper for them to make high demands. During this period, they will have fluctuating moods, and they should try their hardest to keep their emotions under good control. They should be on guard against getting involved in friends' troubles. In this month, it is not proper for them to argue with or talk back to their spouses or lovers. Children may have a very strong desire for material possession, and there will also be some emotional troubles.

-6th month (Wei 未月, Ram's month)
(July 7th to August 6th, 2001)

The prospects for this month are full of twists and turns. In their career, there will be an unexpected development. There will be rumors, trouble and resistance, so they should aim for development in other places; it is not proper to quietly stay in the original work sphere. This is a very good time for making a move and transfer. Wealth can be sought afar. Moreover, there is more than one opportunity. But there are also losses with lucky gains, so they must be fully prepared. In terms of feelings, an old relation might be mended.

-7th month (Shen 申月, Monkey's month)
(August 7th to September 6th, 2001)

In this month, the fluctuation in emotions has not yet subsided, so couples should try to avoid quarrels. Otherwise there might be billows in the sea of love, and it will be too late to repent when the real separation comes. Husband and wife should be candid and honest with each other, and they should be on guard against going to extremes. In addition they should also take care that their spouses do not suffer unexpected accidents, especially during child delivery. There must be a clear separation between public and private in-

terests. And they should guard against disasters pertaining to sex traps.

-8th month *(You 酉月, Rooster's month)* *(September 7th to October 7th, 2001)*

There is some improvement in emotional troubles that have lasted for over a month. They should pay attention to personal images, and should be very cautious when making public speeches, keeping in mind that mishaps often come out of careless remarks. In career, it is possible that some commercial disputes may take place or there may be a loss of customers. If they can have their impatient or rash moods under good control, it will seem perfect. They are all right in health, but they should look after their elders at home. There may be possibilities to attend funerals. The young people should be encouraged.

-9th month *(Shu 戌月, Dog's month)* *(October 8th to November 6th, 2001)*

There is a saying: Laborious work will often fail to set the flowers in blossom, while casually planted willows often promise a shady coziness. This indicates that the more anxious the pursuit, the less fruitful the result; the joy will often come

as a surprise. Luck in the household is good with nice harmony and handsome income. Problems in love are settled. In this month there will be significant advances in work, yet they must give cautious treatment to the gossip and rumors, and should not get entangled in troubles. There are friends lending a helping hand, solving problems and disputes. And now it is favorable to open up new territories and create new ideas and notions.

-10th month (Hai 亥月, Pig's month)
(November 7th to December 6th, 2001)

There is some improvement for the prospects of this month. The deadlock at work can be broken again, difficulties can be overcome, and perilous situations will become safe and sound. But this month is not the proper time to open up new horizons in business. They should not get indulged in wine and sex, let alone extramarital love affairs.

-11th month (Zi 子月, Rat's month)
(December 7th, 2001 to January 4th, 2002)

The prospects for this month are not very good. More often than not, there will be unpredictable clouds and storms, and a rather confusing mixture of luck and mishaps. Fortune and disaster

will alternate their appearances with huge billows surging forward. Therefore they should be on very cautious guard. The more calm and composed they appear, the more trust will be placed in them. Feelings regarding children may put them into an annoying preoccupation. In addition, great care must be taken in dealing with matters of feelings in order not to be deceived by beautiful faces or honey words, otherwise there will be endless future troubles.

-12th month (Chou 丑月, Ox's month) (January 5th to February 3rd, 2002)

There is quite an obvious improvement in the prospects for this month, and the worries in feelings will soon come to an end. Although troubles are unavoidable, there will be steady progress in work. The pity is that luck in money making is mediocre, promising no great gains. During this period, they must pay close attention to health. Negligence might bring them to the hospital for an operation. At the same time, they should be on guard against theft at home.

RAM

*Forecasts by month for those born
in the Year of the Ram*

1907, 1919, 1931, 1943, 1955, 1967, 1979, 1991

-1st month (Yin 寅月, Tiger's month)
(February 4th to March 4th, 2001)

The spring has come back to the land, and everything has taken on a new look. During this month there are auspicious stars shining high above, and everything will be gratifying. People born in the Year of the Ram will have good luck in making money, but a drastic drop will follow

a quick rise. Is spite of that, it is wealth after all. Their persistence in work will solve problems and developments will be smooth. There will be a happy and glorious promotion. It will be a rich and colorful life emotionally, but it is necessary to go on a diet, so as to balance health and happiness.

-2nd month (Mao 卯月, Rabbit's month)
(March 5th to April 4th, 2001)

The prospects for this month are still smooth. There will be sages to guide or help in their work. If they can grasp the opportunity, they will experience a meteoric rise, as if soaring on the wings of a cyclone. During this period it is very easy to be on intimate terms with persons of the opposite sex. But they should let their love travel on the right track, and romance should be kept for their spouse or lover. They should keep away from extramarital love affairs, so as not to draw fire onto themselves.

-3rd month (Chen 辰月, Dragon's month)
(April 5th to May 4th, 2001)

The prospects for this month are a mixture of auspicious and inauspicious elements with occasional fluctuations. It is not really easy to earn money, which in turn will bring about troubles. Difficulties are followed by facilities, and mishaps will turn into fortune. However, wealth is accompanied by hardship. This month is advancing with constant solutions to difficult problems. Therefore, no negligence can be allowed. In work new problems will pop up unexpectedly. But if they are treated with caution, there should be no great problems. During this period, they should never indulge themselves in the gratification of sexual desire and enjoyment, otherwise there will be disasters.

-4th month (Si 巳月, Snake's month)
(May 5th to June 4th, 2001)

There will be great improvements in the prospects for this month. Troubles at work can all be solved, and things will go smoothly. They might obtain something unexpected. They are likely to gain profits during the opening and changing period of the business; they should

have a firm grasp of the good occasion. During this period, they should try to connect more with their customers or try to open up new markets.

-5th month (Wu 午月, Horse's month)
(June 5th to July 6th, 2001)

Luck in money making this month is very good, so they may go on with careful schemes and elaborate designs to make investments, either in local or other places. There will be chances to make money. There will be gains in investments, securities and foreign currencies. During this month it is the performance of their subordinates that causes mental fatigue and efforts.

-6th month (Wei 未月, Ram's month)
(July 7th to August 6th, 2001)

This is a month with rather good prospects, and there are also sages coming to help. Developments at work are fairly satisfactory, and luck in making money is not bad. However there is some resistance in the development of feelings; there are many undercurrents surging here and there – so great are the pains involved in love. If separated geographically, there may be appreciation shown from people of the opposite sex. In this case, they should be on guard against the third

person taking advantage. In addition, they should also take good care lest the children might suffer unexpected injuries.

-7th month (Shen 申月, Monkey's month) (August 7th to September 6th, 2001)

The prospects for this month are rather capricious. Surrounded by delays and troubles in work, they are bustling about with few results. However the problems are not shown but hidden and only exposed very slowly. Now it is the right time for outward development, either a work transfer or new projects. They must take precautions when going outside. They should pay special attention to personal belongings, giving no show of their money to avoid theft. Regarding health, they should pay attention to the hygiene of foods and drinks.

-8th month (You 酉月, Rooster's month) (September 7th to October 7th, 2001)

The prospects for this month show a great improvement, full of vitality and sunshine; "out of the depth of misfortune comes bliss." Although there are occasional hindrances, they can be overcome. And there will be new breakthroughs, the busier the better. It is a favorable time for

dynamic actions rather than quiet observations. There will be some rivals in work and there will be troubles. But there will be a smooth income, though the handling of finances requires caution. All accounts should be clearly settled as soon as possible without delay to avoid endless future troubles.

-9th month (Shu 戌月, Dog's month)
(October 8th to November 6th, 2001)

The prospects for this month are steady with no great fluctuations. They will have achievements, hence praises. They should try to stick to their posts and devote themselves to their work. They should not try to set a high demand for side income to avoid suffering a tragic loss. On the other hand, they should not be too stubborn about the difficult problems regarding feelings and love, which may be settled this month. They might try to seek pleasure in a cozy and romantic atmosphere with a candle-lit dinner. There is good luck at the homestead.

-10th month (Hai 亥月, Pig's month)
(November 7th to December 6th, 2001)

The prospects for this month are rather strong, as if the sun is shining at its zenith, with a cloudless sky that extends for thousands of miles. There is competition in their work, but there are still great opportunities for achievements. There may come the joy of getting a promotion with certain power and influence. They should grasp this opportunity. Young people may have great progress in their studies. If they take examinations during this period, they will have great successes. However, care must be taken so members of the family don't suffer from unexpected mishaps.

-11th month (Zi 子月, Rat's month)
(December 7th, 2001 to January 4th, 2002)

The prospects for this month are full of twists and turns, and there are signs of fluctuation with a sudden change in the situation. There is resistance, accompanied with delays and losses, and they should be wary. Luck for making money is also fluctuating. It is not proper to gamble or to invest, and they should not take any adventur-

ous actions. In terms of their business, they should ensure that customers are not grabbed away by others to avoid suffering a defeat on the verge of victory.

-12th month (Chou 丑月, Ox's month)
(January 5th to February 3rd, 2002)

This month they are not in a very good mood, and they may make some mistakes with investments. They should not be too prejudiced lest relatives and friends should be resentful and irritated, thus putting themselves in an isolated predicament. While in their work, there are huge billows surging forward with great shocking power, but in spite of their busy social schedule, their great efforts bring hardly any solid gains. Luck in earning side income is not very good, so it is not proper to gamble or to invest. In matters of feelings, they will experience a gust of spring breeze: sweet, warm and cozy.

MONKEY

Forecasts by month for those born in the Year of the Monkey

1920, 1932, 1944, 1956, 1968, 1980, 1992

-1st month (Yin 寅月, Tiger's month)
(February 4th to March 4th, 2001)

The prospects for this month are rather mediocre, which does not signify a very good beginning. There are problems in this month's work while there are no auspicious stars in the Destiny Palace that may help to solve their prob-

156

lems. People born in the Year of the Monkey should be mentally prepared. As far as career is concerned, there are both internal worries and external troubles, and luck in making money is also rather obscure. During this period, they should never act upon impulse so as to avoid a rupture in feelings.

-2nd month (Mao 卯月, Rabbit's month) (March 5th to April 4th, 2001)

Luck in making money for this month is very good, which has already swept away the problems of the last month. There will be significant advances in career development, with many achievements and elaborate designs. There are opportunities to make money both locally and in other places. They should guard against possible burdens or troubles brought about by some fair-weather friends. In this month there is a broken Wealth Robbing Star. So it is not proper to warrant for, or lend money to other people. Unmarried people may come across a warm, generous and romantic person of the opposite sex in life, but those married people should take great care in coping with the situation, for the temptation is really difficult to resist.

-3rd month (Chen 辰月, Dragon's month)
(April 5th to May 4th, 2001)

Those born in the Year of the Monkey do not
have excellent prospects for this year in general,
but in this month they have moments with powerful momentum. In career, they have new opportunities for development, outward expansion
and the opening of new markets, as well as for
work transfer. There will be a strong desire for
investment, but there will be very great ups and
downs. Any careless action may bring about
losses as a result. But luck in money making is
good, and investments may bring gains. There
will be new sweet and cozy emotional developments. There is a great improvement in health.
But there may occur troubles between friends.

-4th month (Si 巳月, Snake's month)
(May 5th to June 4th, 2001)

The prospects for this month are paradoxical
with undercurrents lurking, so they must con-
solidate their work to avoid a situation in which
a single mistake may bring total defeat. During
this period, they must pay due attention to the
performance of their subordinates. What worries them most is the unsteady performance of
their subordinates' work. It will be easy to get

into trouble by making improper remarks, so they must be very cautious when making a speech. Luck in making money is poor, so it is not proper to gamble. They are all right in health, but they should never get into the habit of eating or drinking too much.

-5th month (Wu 午月, Horse's month)
(June 5th to July 6th, 2001)

In this month, luck in making money is excellent, with abundant sources for income. But at the end of the month, it is not proper to make side income. It is better to stop before it is too late. When signing documents they have to be extremely cautious; there may be some deceptions. They tend to make some improper remarks, so they must be careful with their speech. There will be great advances in matters of feelings, with a sweet and cozy atmosphere. Those who do not have a boyfriend or girlfriend may have many opportunities to meet the ideal person of the opposite sex. While they should not make bold advances, they must build up their courage to express their sincere intentions and kindly feelings, so as not to miss a good opportunity. Regarding health, they must pay attention to bronchitis.

-6th month (Wei 未月, Ram's month)
(July 7th to August 6th, 2001)

The prospects for this month are improving greatly, with a bright moon shinning high above. The development of their career is on the right track, but constant and further efforts should be made. During this period they should give heed to as many different opinions as they can and make more friends of different types and from different layers. They must choose people for a job according to their abilities, without sticking to one pattern only. Otherwise, there can hardly be any great success. Luck in making money makes a turn for the better, and investments may bring about profits. During this period, it is not proper to hanker after side income.

-7th month (Shen 申月, Monkey's month)
(August 7th to September 6th, 2001)

In this month the prospects make a sharp turn for the worse. There are problems in planning and in action. First of all there must be mental preparation, lest they should be unprepared and at a loss for what to do. Their career development will be like rowing a boat against the current, difficult to progress but easy to regress. Therefore, constant endeavors are absolutely nec-

essary. Because the Fortune Star is broken this month, it is better for them to keep their hands away from investing or gambling for the time being so as not to fall into a terrible fix. In addition, it is also necessary to guard against robbery. They should remember that safety comes first. They are not in ideal health, so they should pay close attention to the hygiene of foods and drinks.

-8th month (You 酉月, Rooster's month) (September 7th to October 7th, 2001)

The prospects for this month are still going well, as if the Sun is shining at its zenith. Advances at work are making headway and the development of their career is going well. They may as well try a multi-dimensional development, because it is very likely to achieve unexpected gains. The prospects and the career development are mutually complementary, so if they can take a good hold of the opportunities, there will surely be a gain in fame and wealth.

-9th month (Shu 戌月, Dog's month) (October 8th to November 6th, 2001)

Now luck in money making is turning for the better, and it is proper to make multi-dimen-

sional investments. In this month sages will come to help, so they are gradually entering a favorable situation. The prospects for this month go upward. At the beginning there will be many hindrances, but the situation is something of an old saying: Laborious work will often fail to set the flowers in blossom, while casually planted willows often promise a shady coziness. Through twists and turns the path is now leading gradually to a favorable status. They will be at an advantageous position at work, but still the solid foundation will have to be laid through their own efforts. And in matters of feelings there are new chances, but they have to take the initiative.

-10th month (Hai 亥月, Pig's month)
(November 7th to December 6th, 2001)

The prospects for this month are turning from bad to worse, with so many hindrances and difficulties, and this is especially obvious in luck of money making. Therefore they must be extremely cautious in dealing with financial issues so as to avoid a great loss of money. At the verge of success their efforts will be of no value if they cannot handle an emergency with both composure and flexibility. During this period they must take the greatest care to play to the score. If they

do not understand how to act according to the circumstances, they will suffer a crushing defeat. There might be love affairs in other places, so they have to be careful, otherwise there will be endless future troubles. There will be diseases in the stomach and intestines, so they have to be careful with their diet.

-11th month (Zi 子月, Rat's month)
(December 7th, 2001 to January 4th, 2002)

Luck in making money is still good, and investment may bring about huge profits. They must remember that they should never show their wealth and money. There are very smooth advances in work. But it is easy to offend mean people. They should try to make concessions to avoid trouble, giving up something may allow greater flexibility for the future. In this month there are auspicious stars shining high in the Destiny Palace of those born in the Monkey year, so they are sound and healthy in body and mind. In matters of feelings there is a warm and sweet congeniality, which may bring about flowers and fruits of love. This is a golden opportunity for marriage. Luck for their children is wonderful, with good reputation and nice profits.

-12th month (Chou 丑月, Ox's month)
(January 5th to February 3rd, 2002)

Although there is nothing special in the prospects for this month, there are quite a lot of inspirations with outstanding creativity. There is much variety in their work, but they can hardly achieve anything without confidence. When traveling or running a business errand they should pay attention to safety, and be on guard against accidents during the journey. In their spare time, after work or school, young people should take part in more activities regarding arts and culture. This may change their fate by developing their potential. During this period, it is not proper to seek side income.

ROOSTER

*Forecasts by month for those born
in the Year of the Rooster*

1909, 1921, 1933, 1945, 1957, 1969, 1981, 1993

*-1st month (Yin 寅月, Tiger's month)
(February 4th to March 4th, 2001)*

This month meets fortunes and welcomes the spring. It is favorable to make a living and make money abroad. Those born in the Year of the Rooster have strong management abilities.

165

Though sometimes they will get into trouble and experience mental pressure, they will have the ability to solve problems. There will be very good luck in making money, but they should only play with small stakes for pleasure. They will have some money left which can be put into their savings. In matters of feelings, things are satisfactory. This is a month of good luck.

-2nd month (Mao 卯月, Rabbit's month) (March 5th to April 4th, 2001)

According to the prospects for this month, they should be on guard against a sudden change. Problems will come from brothers, partners or friends. They should be careful, for there will be rumors and slanders. At this time it is better to be bustling about, the busier the better. Difficulties will come first and then will be followed by smooth sailing, and the mishaps will turn into fortune and dangers into safety. There are some problems in health, and it is quite possible for them to catch epidemics. They must pay close attention to their dietary habits.

-3rd month (Chen 辰月, Dragon's month)
(April 5th to May 4th, 2001)

The prospects for this month are improving significantly, with a gradual removal of pressure from work. This is especially true of luck in making money. During this period it is possible to make profits by investment, but there lie some undercurrents; they cannot afford to totally relax. They must be very careful financially, or they can never expect to accumulate anything decent. There will be some new developments in matters of feelings, but it is hard to predict the consequence. They must pay attention to their diet, guarding against those foods that might be detrimental to their health.

-4th month (Si 巳月, Snake's month)
(May 5th to June 4th, 2001)

The prospects for this month are smooth and flamboyant; work is done with facility, and there are sages of the opposite sex coming to help. Luck in making money is excellent; there will be income from various sources. However, the family expenditure is also big. They should never be too greedy for success without considering the

elements for possible failure. In addition, they should be financially cautious. When the Red Phoenix Star comes along, married couples will enjoy each other and there is a good promise of marriage for the unmarried lovers.

-5th month (Wu 午月, Horse's month)
(June 5th to July 6th, 2001)

There appears a slight drop in the prospects for this month; many things are delayed, thus affecting the advances of their work. Possible income will slip away; it is not proper to make investments, let alone speculations. There is some disturbance in the household, but with timely help and support from a spouse, they can settle the issues together. They are not in very good health, and headaches, insomnia and heart troubles will appear. And during this period, there will be emotional problems such as worries and irritations.

-6th month (Wei 未月, Ram's month)
(July 7th to August 6th, 2001)

The prospects for this month do not show a splendid auspice, but compared with that of the last month, they are smoother and more fluent. Those born in the Year of the Rooster are generally in a good mood for work, and there will be gains and losses in their career. If they can develop their career whole-heartedly, there will soon be ideal results. Nevertheless, they should be on guard against troubles between people. There will be social gatherings among friends jostling with temptations of banquets and beauties, wealth and money, so they must be on guard against bad friends and sexual traps.

-7th month (Shen 申月, Monkey's month)
(August 7th to September 6th, 2001)

The prospects for this month are like a calm sea, but undercurrents are lurking. So they should be cautious in investments and speculation transactions. There might be troubles so they have to guard against mistakes, and keep in mind that accidents may occur anytime. Therefore, they should sharpen their vigilance. It is not at all proper to gamble. Special care must be taken to guard against dangers caused by water. In mat-

ters of feelings, they will be drawn into an emotional vortex, so they must cope with the situation cautiously. If bad feelings can be detected, it is better to back totally out as early as possible.

-8th month (You 酉月, Rooster's month)
(September 7th to October 7th, 2001)

They will face challenges this month, especially in their career, so they must do their best. The tough problems can be solved and the solutions to difficult issues may win respect and power. Luck in making money is not very good. They must have patience and perseverance, and they must be very cautious in handling financial problems. They should never borrow money so as not to get bogged down, which may lead to lawsuits.

-9th month (Shu 戌月, Dog's month)
(October 8th to November 6th, 2001)

The prospects have a great improvement this month. In career, there will be sages coming to their support. They will also have support and cooperation from their colleagues. The prospects are generally steady, with finances looking better than career. When going out they should be extremely careful and guard against unexpected

accidents. The young people will make progress in their studies during this period.

-10th month (Hai 亥月, Pig's month)
(November 7th to December 6th, 2001)

The prospects for this month will be rather fluctuating. In their career they will come across hindrances and difficulties. The difficult problems they encounter will surely be solved. For the young people, their schoolwork will regress. Fortunately, luck in money will be good and there will be no financial difficulties. They must now pay attention to family happiness, and take good care of family members and remind them that they must be on guard against unexpected accidents as well as diseases of liver and gallbladder.

-11th month (Zi 子月, Rat's month)
(December 7th, 2001 to January 4th, 2002)

In this month they will face challenges. They must cautiously cope with the fluctuating situation. In their work they will face great challenges. They must stick to their posts and duties, taking no hasty or rash actions, and the proper thing to do is to be tolerant. At the same time they must be on guard against those ill characters who may

hit them when they are down. Therefore, they must take very cautious measures. During this period they should try all they can to improve interpersonal relations, for this has something to do with the final success or failure of their career. Poor luck in making money and the troubles in matters of feelings need to be treated with calm and composure.

-12th month (Chou 丑月, Ox's month) (January 5th to February 3rd, 2002)

At the end of the year comes good luck that is worth celebrating. The wonderful luck regarding both career and finance promise an enjoyment of the fruits of achievement. Their power and position are rising when they are busy bustling about, yet there still may be resistance in career. Fortunately there appear auspicious stars in the Destiny Palace, so if they have due vigilance, perilous dangers may become blissful peace. Though money and wealth come and go in a rush, they will end up with good income. However, they should keep their money inconspicuous to avoid disasters of robbery.

DOG

Forecasts by month for those born
in the Year of the Dog

1910, 1922, 1934, 1946, 1958, 1970, 1982, 1994

-1st month (Yin 寅月, Tiger's month)
(February 4th to March 4th, 2001)

During the period of the New Spring prospects are not so good, so it is necessary to be mentally prepared. However, your friends will be able to ease your worries and dispel your depression. There will be a very great expenditure in social

settings, including banquets and entertainment. Money will come and go with a lot of waste. So there should be a good plan for expenses. They should be on a careful diet because they are not very good in health, and they must avoid harm to the stomach and intestines. During this period they ought to be careful with their money and be cautious in investment. In matters of feelings, the sunshine will add interest and delight.

-2nd month (Mao 卯月, Rabbit's month) (March 5th to April 4th, 2001)

The prospects for this month are not really auspicious, but compared with that of the last month they are a little bit better. The pressure of work will gradually decrease, but in this month it is not proper to hold wedding ceremonies that may be met with some resistance. And there will be some improvement in health. And they should also pay close attention to the health of the middle-aged and the elderly at home. Luck in making money is improving, so they may play with small stakes for fun and delight, which may bring some unexpected gains.

-3rd month (Chen 辰月, Dragon's month)
(April 5th to May 4th, 2001)

The prospects for this month are unpredictable.
In work there are occasional difficulties, and
there are people who will talk behind your back
and set traps. During this period it is more proper
to take the defense rather than launch an offense.
They should take no rash actions. They must
remind their spouse or lover of the importance
of guarding against mistakes in documents and
contracts, and robbery as well. They must be
careful with the hygiene of their diet to avoid
catching contagious diseases.

-4th month (Si 巳月, Snake's month)
(May 5th to June 4th, 2001)

The prospects for this month are rather smooth
and flamboyant. The difficulties and problems
that have plagued their work for a long time
could all be readily overcome. The external
temptations are great, and there appears a strong
desire to create, expand and develop outward.
They itch for change, and this is the right time
for action. In matters of feelings there will be
new developments. They should never start any
unduly romance or sexual games. They should
pay close attention to health, and they should

not be exhausted by their work. And if they have a disease, they should never delay treatment.

-5th month (Wu 午月, Horse's month)
(June 5th to July 6th, 2001)

The prospects for this month are quite smooth, so it is favorable to go outside to make money and profits. And they should pay attention to the good tidings from afar, and take a firm grasp of the opportunities. During this period, investment may bring profits and they may consider the purchase of real estate. There will be new developments in relations with their spouse, lover or sweetheart. It will be a very rich and colorful love life.

-6th month (Wei 未月, Ram's month)
(July 7th to August 6th, 2001)

Prospects fall back this month, and their career will face grave challenges. Open-mindedness and depression will take turns alternating. They will be busy in their work, but their efforts will be spent in vain. The biggest problems come from interpersonal relations, with some people deliberately picking on faults and making trouble. The progress is slow in matters of feel-

ings, and it seems that some force is holding it back. At the present, they have to take the strategy of patience and tolerance.

-7th month (Shen 申月, Monkey's month)
(August 7th to September 6th, 2001)

The prospects for this month are capricious, with crises lurking. They should not be reckless. In career, hard work is required, but there are troubles. They should try to approach problems in person rather than relying on others so there is not a delay in work or business. They also want to guard against suffering losses due to the betrayal of others who took advantage of an opportunity. There is danger on the way, and the situation is serious. They can never adopt a casual attitude or let down their guard, for this might be disastrous. There is an increase in attraction and charm, and in confidence this month. It is favorable for them to enjoy sweet love. And the situation with their children is improving, which will be a great comfort.

-8th month (You 酉月, Rooster's month)
(September 7th to October 7th, 2001)

The prospects for this month are improving slightly, and the crisis in work is also abating. Things are going smooth, but they have to be treated with care. Fortunately they are in good health. There might be some troubles at home with differences in opinion and each side holding an argument, which pushes them into a bad mood. In matters of love, there is a big fluctuation, and there might come a crack, so they have to try to mend the relationship with great care.

-9th month (Shu 戌月, Dog's month)
(October 8th to November 6th, 2001)

The prospects for this month involve lots of trouble and disputes. In this case they had better avoid a tit for tat struggle that will bring about no gains for either side. In career there will appear a situation with conflicts and contradictions. Externally, there will be new opponents who are very strong and powerful. So they really need patience and will power, and must pull out all stops in their work. Sages will also come to their help. In this month they have to remember that there is only a very tiny gap

between a friend and a lover, and they should lead an honest and clean life.

-10th month (Hai 亥月, Pig's month)
(November 7th to December 6th, 2001)

There is no great improvement in the prospects for this month. Though at the beginning of the month there will be some resistance, the situation will gradually enter a favorable phase, with great improvement in career and luck in making money. But they have to be careful with their letters and documents. Too much talk will often lead to mistake. Their health is not very ideal. Besides paying attention to their diet and living habits, they should also try to avoid the harm done to their health by alcohol and foods.

-11th month (Zi 子月, Rat's month)
(December 7th, 2001 to January 4th, 2002)

The prospects for this month are like the fine weather after rain. The bad luck that has lasted for months has been swept clean. So there will be great undertakings in career, with relatives and friends coming to their help. There will be good progress in young people's studies, but they should not get be elated or beside themselves. They should also take care not to catch cold, protecting their lungs and bronchi.

-12th month (Chou 丑月, Ox's month)
(January 5th to February 3rd, 2002)

In this month the prospects for the year have undercurrents lurking, so people born in the Year of the Dog must be on guard against sudden changes. Such fluctuating prospects with sharp rises and drastic drops tend to be erratic at the end of the year. There may come a sudden tempest. So they must be very careful and cautious in every aspect, guarding against accidents. Luck for children is good. Special guard must be taken against extramarital love affairs and a change in feelings. In addition, they must refrain themselves from bold and unconstrained gambling.

PIG

*Forecasts by month for those born
in the Year of the Pig*

1911, 1923, 1935, 1947, 1959, 1971, 1983, 1995

*-1st month (Yin 寅月, Tiger's month)
(February 4th to March 4th, 2001)*

At the beginning of the New Year, the prospects are like wild storms with resistance at every step forward. Laborious work brings hardly any fortune that can be enjoyed. So they must act very

cautiously. Especially in work, they have to be careful because superiors might be rather fault picking. When they try to solve or settle difficult problems, they should try all they can to turn an unfavorable situation into a better one. There are obstacles in matters of love, with some hidden reefs underneath. The progress is slow. They must have patience, and on many occasions they will feel lonely this month.

-2nd month (Mao 卯月, Rabbit's month)
(March 5th to April 4th, 2001)

The prospects for this month are steadily rising, so there are achievements in their work. And there are some helping forces coming from without, and many difficult passes will be broken. But during this period, it is very easy to cause troubles, which they can avoid by not making improper remarks. Luck in making money is very good, with an abundant regular income, but the side income is rather capricious. Luck in matters of love is pretty nice, romantic and warm, but there will appear rivals. A great comfort is that there will be sages coming to help when they go outside.

-3rd month (Chen 辰月, Dragon's month)
(April 5th to May 4th, 2001)

In this month luck in making money is mediocre, so they must be cautious in dealing with
finance to prevent money from leaking away.
They should never let their money be an eye-
catching show to avoid inviting disasters of robbery. There will be many hindrances in work,
so they must try to concentrate on the solution
of those problems rather than poking a long nose
into other people's business. They might, however, gain profits in far away places. They may
obtain profits by settling difficult problems in
remote places or coming from afar. Nevertheless, the profits may also bring along troubles.
The health situation shows an omen of bloodshed or hospitalization for an operation. Therefore they must rest well and be on cautious guard
against falling sick.

-4th month (Si 巳月, Snake's month)
(May 5th to June 4th, 2001)

The prospects for this month show undesirable
things coming in one after another. The
projects will come to a sudden stop without
any known reason. They must be mentally

prepared to handle it. They must take care when going outside, and they should not get into an impulsive argument or dispute. Instead, they should pay attention to traffic safety, for there might be unexpected accidents. In terms of relations with lovers or spouses, it is very likely there may appear a third person.

-5th month (Wu 午月, Horse's month)
(June 5th to July 6th, 2001)

There will be some new breakthroughs in their work. They should let change take place, accepting new chances and fate. That will testify to the saying: Laborious work will often fail to set the flowers in blossom, while casually planted willows will often promise a shady coziness. In addition, they should not have any sense of loss or compunction. They should be careful while traveling outside, driving or crossing the street. In matters of love, their luck is excellent, even small disagreements may bring about delights and interests. Their spouses are very inspiring, so they should let them bring their abilities into full play.

-6th month (Wei 未月, Ram's month)
(July 7th to August 6th, 2001)

This month they have extraordinary momentum, and that is the moment to attain fame. They have good manners when dealing with people and are respected for their problem-solving skills. They have a quick mind and lots of valuable ideas, which shows superb ability. No problems will overcome them. They have a strong desire for investment and a wise judgement. In terms of feelings, there are some emotional obstacles that do not involve a third person, so time and patience are necessary for solving problems.

-7th month (Shen 申月, Monkey's month)
(August 7th to September 6th, 2001)

The prospects this month are sometimes smooth, but other times stagnant, which is quite irritating. The greater the difficulties, the greater the achievements. Looking forward will leave people to a better mood. There will be some disturbance at home, so they should be careful to protect family members from getting into disasters with bloodshed. Their relationship with their loved one may experience some somber moments with inevitable quarrels, and they should also guard against undue love affairs.

-8th month (You 酉月, Rooster's month)
(September 7th to October 7th, 2001)

In this month those born in the Pig year are resolute and wise in their career, with both fame and gain, just like the sun shining at its zenith. The change in this month is satisfactory. They are in excellent standing financially, and they will get help from their best friends. In love, things will shift from difficult to easy. After traveling on a road full of twists and turns, a wonderland will appear. The pursuit of romance may lead them to a sweetheart they will fall in love with at first sight.

-9th month (Shu 戌月, Dog's month)
(October 8th to November 6th, 2001)

In this month they will have a good reputation and will be respected by others. It is a good time for them to be representatives of public opinion, and they will be famous through activities of public welfare. At this time it is not proper to get involved in speculation, for it will run too great a risk. Moreover, they should also be cautious in investment. There must be good plans for expenditure, so that money can be spent whenever appropriate and necessary. At the same time they

should try to have nothing to do with unduly obtained wealth and money. Otherwise, they will surely get into troubles.

-10th month (Hai 亥月, Pig's month) (November 7th to December 6th, 2001)

The prospects for this month suffer a disastrous decline, boding ill rather than well. So they must remember that too much talk will often bring about mistakes. Taking precautions is absolutely necessary, and they cannot afford to allow any negligence. There seem to be a lot of chances in career, investment and finance, but more often than not the seemingly grand roads will be pits when they get there. They should never lend money to others, nor should they be the warrantors. They must pay attention to unexpected injuries, especially when taking part in outdoor activities; they must be on guard against unintentional hits to avoid accidents. The elderly people should take good hold of the handrail when going up and down stairs.

-11th month (Zi 子月, Rat's month)
(December 7th, 2001 to January 4th, 2002)

The prospects for this month are smooth and fluent, so a sinister situation will turn into an auspicious one. There are so many things that can be done in their career, and luck in making money is also changing for the better, thus investments will bring profits. There can hardly be any breakthroughs in matters of feelings, so they should let things take their natural course. If there are chances for outings, they should enjoy themselves and relax their nerves. But their spouses can hardly be happy when going on an outing. They themselves are not in very good health, and they should be careful with their stomach and intestines.

-12th month (Chou 丑月, Ox's month)
(January 5th to February 3rd, 2002)

There is a great improvement in money making, so there will be abundant sources for income. The good fortune has penetrated to the soul, thus things can be handled with great facility, promising good chances and achievements. Gains and profits are still in the far distance, so it is proper to go out to other places to seek wealth. Traveling away from home will do them good. As a matter of fact, they cannot stop at all this month; they are so busy bustling about. But it is important that activities should bring about good results. It is easy for them to neglect their spouses or lovers, as they are usually tired, in a bad temper and quarrelsome. So it is inevitable to be at odds with one another.

1	7	☆ make offerings to ancestors; baths; visit friends; marriage; sign contracts; launch business
M	●	✘ *pray for happiness; lay foundations*
2	8	☆ make offerings; visit friends; travel; receive payment; new clothes; visit friends; funerals
T	○	✘ *sow crops; mourning; install gravestone*
3	9	☆ install home appliances; sow crops; sign contracts engagements; move house; study
W	●	✘ *kitchen work; repair fishing nets*
4	10	☆ make offerings; garden work; repair paths; end mourning; lay foundations; install home appliances
T	●	✘ *prepare wedding bed; hairstyling; dig wells*
5	11	☆ make offerings to gods; baths; manicure babies; housecleaning; install roof; new clothes ❑ Slight Cold
F	○	✘ *travel; prepare wedding bed; buy land*
6	12	☆ make offerings to gods; visit friends; marriage; install roof; adopt pets; kitchen work
S	○	✘ *travel; sow crops; christen boat; end mourning*
7	13	☆ pray for happiness; make offerings; marriage; move house; funerals; hunt and fish; lay foundations; install roof
S	○	✘ *install home appliances; hunt; fishing*
8	14	☆ demolish old house/wall unlucky day: no important activities
M	●	✘ *lay foundations; funerals; make wine*
9	15	☆ make offerings; open stores; make wine; adopt pets; funerals; lay foundations
T	○	✘ *dig wells; prepare wedding bed*
10	16	☆ Lunar Eclipse unlucky day: no important activities
W	●	✘ *legal trial; demolish, lay foundations*
11	17	☆ make offerings; housecleaning; hairstyling; new clothes; kitchen work; hunt and fish
T	○	✘ *move house; payment*
12	18	☆ study; pray for fertility; install roof; visit friends; dig wells; baths; new clothes; kitchen work
F	●	✘ *end mourning; give dowries; sow crops; cut trees*
13	19	☆ make offerings; new clothes; prepare wedding bed; adopt pets; hairstyling; funerals
S	○	✘ *open stores; kitchen work*
14	20	☆ make offerings; sign contracts; business; buy houses
S	○	✘ *pray for fertility; funerals; receive payment*
15	21	☆ study; engagements; marriage; move house kitchen work; baths; install roof
M	●	✘ *make offerings; travel; lay foundations; funerals*

● lucky day   ○ neutral day   ● unlucky day   ❑ 24 solar terms
☆ auspicious activity   ✘ inauspicious activity

16	22	☆ make offerings; receive payment; engagements; study; business; repair fishing nets
T	○	✖ *dig wells; end mourning; funerals*
17	23	☆ marriage; make offerings; repair paths; move house; prepare wedding bed; install roof
W	○	✖ *open stores; repair fishing nets*
18	24	☆ engagements; adopt pets; pray for happiness; marriage; install roof; lay foundations
T	●	✖ *make wine; sow crops; travel; end mourning*
19	25	☆ travel; baths; hairstyling; funerals; hunt and fish; prepare wedding bed; install roof
F	○	✖ *open stores; build dams*
20	26	☆ demolish old house/wall unlucky day: no important activities ❑ Great Cold
S	●	✖ *engagements; marriage; sign contracts; legal trial*
21	27	☆ make offerings; travel; new clothes; hairstyling; install roof; move house; sow crops
S	●	✖ *engagements; prepare wedding bed*
22	28	☆ study; marriage; engagements; marriage; loft work; funerals; build dams
M	○	✖ *hunt and fish; sow crops*
23	29	☆ demolish old house/wall unlucky day: no important activities
T	●	✖ *kitchen work; hairstyling; deliver goods*
24	1st	☆ Year of the Snake: God of Fortune in the South;
W	◐	✖ *hairstyling; marriage; funerals; end mourning*
25	2	☆ make offerings; pray for happiness; baths; move house; travel; new clothes; prepare wedding bed
T	●	✖ *buy houses; buy land*
26	3	☆ new clothes; install altar; baths; hairstyling; open stores
F	○	✖ *lay foundations; fishing; funerals*
27	4	☆ visit friends; engagements; install roof; funerals; travel; move house; business
S	○	✖ *make offerings; repair fishing nets*
28	5	☆ make offerings; adopt pets; study; install home appliances; install roof; engagements; funerals
S	○	✖ *make wine; lay foundations; dig wells*
29	6	☆ hunt and fish ; funerals; install gravestone; repair paths
M	○	✖ *build dams; drain water*
30	7	☆ engagements; marriage; install furnaces; install roof; install gravestone; make wine
T	○	✖ *travel; end mourning; christen boat; legal trial*
31	8	☆ make offerings; baths; new clothes; travel; study; housecleaning; hunt and fish; cut trees
W	●	✖ *bathroom work; install home appliances; marriage*

● lucky day ○neutral day ●unlucky day ❑ 24 solar terms
☆ auspicious activity ✖ inauspicious activity

191

1 T	*9* ●	☆ demolish old house/wall; make offerings; unlucky day: no important activities ✖ *acupuncture; sow crops*
2 F	*10* ◐	☆ make offerings; pray for happiness; funerals; install roof; housecleaning; sign contracts; hunt and fish ✖ *kitchen work; prepare wedding bed*
3 S	*11* ●	☆ install home appliances; sow crops; sign contracts unlucky day: no important activities ✖ *hairstyling; legal trial*
4 S	*12* ○	☆ open stores; business; interior decoration ❒ Beginning of Spring ✖ *buy houses; buy land; legal trial*
5 M	*13* ●	☆ baths; housecleaning unlucky day: no important activities ✖ *marriage; engagements; mourning*
6 T	*14* ○	☆ make offerings to gods; visit friends; marriage; install roof; adopt pets; kitchen work ✖ *repair fishing nets; garden work*
7 W	*15* ○	☆ pray for happiness; make offerings; marriage; travel; hunt and fish; lay foundations; study; new clothes ✖ *make wine; make preserves*
8 T	*16* ●	☆ visit friends; engagements; new clothes; install roof; prepare wedding bed; adopt pets ✖ *make offerings; build dams*
9 F	*17* ◐	☆ make offerings; open stores; visit friends; medical check; adopt pets; funerals; travel ✖ *dig wells; dig ponds; legal trial*
10 S	*18* ○	☆ make offerings to gods; make offerings to ancestors; visit friends; prepare wedding bed; new clothes ✖ *deliver goods; mourning*
11 S	*19* ●	☆ make offerings to gods/to ancestors; housecleaning unlucky day: no important activities ✖ *sow crops; travel*
12 M	*20* ◐	☆ make offerings; pray for fertility; install roof; visit friends; dig wells; baths; new clothes; kitchen work ✖ *kitchen work; bathroom work*
13 T	*21* ●	☆ make offerings; new clothes; study; travel; open stores; adopt pets; funerals ✖ *hairstyling; new clothes*
14 W	*22* ●	☆ make offerings; pray for happiness unlucky day: no important activities ✖ *prepare wedding bed; buying houses*
15 T	*23* ●	☆ make offerings; prepare wedding bed; sign contracts; business; funerals ✖ *sow crops; christen boat*

● lucky day   ○ neutral day   ● unlucky day   ❒ 24 solar terms
☆ auspicious activity   ✖ inauspicious activity

192

16	24	☆ make offerings to ancestors; study; make offerings to gods; disinfection
F	○	✖ *repair fishing nets; end mourning*
17	25	☆ make offerings; baths unlucky day: no important activities
S	●	✖ *marriage; funerals; install door*
18	26	☆ make offerings; study; adopt child; move house; lay foundations; engagements ❏ Rain Water
S	●	✖ *irrigation; drain water; cut trees*
19	27	☆ new clothes; prepare wedding bed; construction; cut trees; funerals; kitchen work
M	○	✖ *legal trial; lay foundations; buy houses*
20	28	☆ sign contracts; business; visit friends; adopt pets; prepare wedding bed
T	○	✖ *marriage; engagements; mourning; adopt pets*
21	29	☆ make offerings; visit friends; hairstyling; medical check; baths; dig ponds; funerals; end mourning
W	●	✖ *garden work; dig ponds; buy houses*
22	30	☆ make offerings; pray for happiness; travel; move house; lay foundations; funerals; prepare wedding bed
T	●	✖ *end mourning; install furnaces; dig wells; funerals*
23	1st	☆ make offerings; paint walls; repair paths unlucky day: no important activities
F	○	✖ *hairstyling; travel; buy houses; funerals*
24	2	☆ make offerings; pray for happiness; visit friends; marriage; open stores; lay foundations; install furnaces
S	●	✖ *buy houses; buy land; bathroom work*
25	3	☆ make offerings; study; visit friends; lay foundations; funerals
S	○	✖ *kitchen work; move house*
26	4	☆ medical check; demolish old house unlucky day: no important activities
M	●	✖ *repair fishing nets; prepare wedding bed*
27	5	☆ make offerings; pray for happiness; sign contracts; lay foundations; funerals; hunt and fish; end mourning
T	○	✖ *make preserves; make wine; dig ponds*
28	6	☆ make offerings; pray for happiness; study; engagements; business; adopt pets; funerals
W	●	✖ *irrigation; drain water; manicure babies*

● lucky day   ○ neutral day   ● unlucky day   ❏ 24 solar terms
☆ auspicious activity   ✖ inauspicious activity

MARCH 2000 / 2nd month of the Snake year

1 T ●	7	☆ make offerings; demolish old house/wall; dig wells unlucky day: no important activities ✖ *legal trial; marriage*
2 F ○	8	☆ make offerings; study; visit friends; launch business; lay foundations; sow crops; medical check ✖ *end mourning; funerals; repair fishing nets*
3 S ○	9	☆ make offerings; travel; prepare wedding bed; irriga- tion; bathroom work; medical check ✖ *sow crops; lay foundations*
4 S ●	10	☆ visit friends; engagements; sign contracts; adopt pets; install roof; funerals; cut trees ✖ *make offerings; install furnaces*
5 M ●	11	☆ make offerings; travel; move house; marriage; lay founda- tions; funerals ❒ Awakening from hibernation ✖ *hairstyling; dig wells; christen boat*
6 T ○	12	☆ travel; hairstyling; baths; do-it-yourself; demolish old house/wall; housecleaning ✖ *buy houses; funerals*
7 W ○	13	☆ make offerings; pray for happiness; study; visit friends; engagements; open stores; adopt pets ✖ *travel; lay foundations; end mourning*
8 T ○	14	☆ make offerings; install furnaces; repair paths; paint walls; business ✖ *repair fishing nets; interior decoration*
9 F ●	15	☆ make offerings; pray for happiness; study; visit friends; marriage; lay foundations; funerals ✖ *end mourning; make wine; make preserves*
10 S ○	16	☆ make offerings; baths; hunt and fish; end mourning; housecleaning; funerals ✖ *irrigation; prepare wedding bed*
11 S ●	17	☆ medical check; demolish old house/wall unlucky day: no important activities ✖ *christen boat*
12 M ●	18	☆ make offerings; pray for happiness; visit friends; travel; lay foundations; marriage; install roof; funerals ✖ *hunt and fish; deliver goods; travel in boat*
13 T ●	19	☆ demolish old house/wall unlucky day: no important activities ✖ *make offerings; install furnaces; funerals*
14 W ○	20	☆ marriage; sign contracts; business; repair fishing nets; sow crops ✖ *kitchen work; install furnaces*
15 T ●	21	☆ make offerings; pray for happiness; study; visit friends; travel; engagements; marriage; lay foundations ✖ *hairstyling; paint walls; manicure babies*

● lucky day ○ neutral day ● unlucky day ❒ 24 solar terms
☆ auspicious activity ✖ inauspicious activity

194

16	22	☆	new clothes; build dams; paint walls; adopt pets
F	◐	✖	*buy houses; make offerings*
17	23	☆	visit friends; travel; repair fishing nets; travel
S	○	✖	*dig wells; lay foundations*
18	24	☆	travel; hairstyling; baths
S	○	✖	*make wine; sow crops; travel; end mourning*
19	25	☆	make offerings; demolish old house/wall
			unlucky day: no important activities
M	●	✖	*lay foundations*
20	26	☆	repair paths; paint walls
			❏ Spring Equinox
T	○	✖	*irrigation; drain water*
21	27	☆	make offerings; pray for happiness; pray for fertility; visit friends; marriage; lay foundations
W	●	✖	*legal trial; christen boat*
22	28	☆	make offerings; study; marriage; move house; hairstyling; end mourning; funerals
T	●	✖	*prepare wedding bed; construction*
23	29	☆	demolish old house/wall
			unlucky day: no important activities
F	●	✖	*sow crops; end mourning*
24	30	☆	make offerings; pray for happiness; travel; engagements; marriage; lay foundations; prepare wedding bed
S	●	✖	*install furnaces; christen boat*
25	1st	☆	make offerings; travel; move house; buy houses;
			unlucky day: no important activities
S	●	✖	*hairstyling; marriage; funerals*
26	2	☆	marriage; hairstyling; engagements; repair fishing nets; hunt and fish; baths; install gravestone
M	○	✖	*buy house/land; funerals*
27	3	☆	make offerings; pray for happiness; study; visit friends; marriage; medical check; open stores
T	●	✖	*paint walls; christen boat*
28	4	☆	engagements; sign contracts; business; lay foundations; build dams; install furnaces
W	●	✖	*make offerings; repair fishing nets; travel; adopt pets*
29	5	☆	visit friends; travel; sign contracts; business; buy houses;
T	○	✖	*make preserves; dig wells*
30	6	☆	travel; hairstyling; repair fishing nets; housecleaning; manicure babies; hunt and fish
F	○	✖	*irrigation; drain water; funerals*
31	7	☆	make offerings; pray for happiness; visit friends; new clothes; open stores; sign contracts
S	●	✖	*legal trial; lay foundations; travel; funerals*

● lucky day ○ neutral day ●unlucky day ❏ 24 solar terms
☆ auspicious activity ✖ inauspicious activity

APRIL 2001 / *3rd month of the Snake year*

1	8	☆ make offerings; repair paths; install roof; interior decoration; end mourning
S	○	✖ *bathroom work; funerals; deliver goods*
2	9	☆ make offerings; pray for happiness; pray for fertility; visit friends; engagements; study
M	●	✖ *sow crops; lay foundations; end mourning; funerals*
3	10	☆ make offerings; pray for happiness; travel; visit friends; hairstyling; repair fishing nets; funerals
T	○	✖ *kitchen work; prepare wedding bed*
4	11	☆ demolish old house/wall unlucky day: no important activities
W	●	✖ *hairstyling; open stores*
5	12	☆ make offerings; medical check; demolish house unlucky day: no important activities ❐ Pure Brightness
T	●	✖ *buy house/land; end mourning*
6	13	☆ baths; repair fishing nets; demolish old house/wall unlucky day: no important activities
F	●	✖ *marriage; end mourning; funerals; buy houses*
7	14	☆ make offerings; pray for happiness; study; visit friends; engagements; marriage; sign contracts
S	●	✖ *repair fishing nets; visit fortuneteller*
8	15	☆ make offerings; receive payment; hunt and fish; install furnaces; end mourning; adopt pets
S	○	✖ *make preserves; make wine*
9	16	☆ visit friends; travel; study; funerals; marriage; sign contracts; business
M	●	✖ *irrigation; make offerings; pray for happiness*
10	17	☆ new clothes; do it yourself; install furnaces; end mourning; funerals; prepare wedding bed
T	○	✖ *legal trial; dig wells; make offerings; drain water*
11	18	☆ make offerings; hairstyling; new clothes; prepare wedding bed; paint walls; hunt and fish
W	○	✖ *lay foundations; bathroom work*
12	19	☆ hairstyling; new clothes; move house unlucky day: no important activities
T	●	✖ *sow crops; travel; bathroom work; marriages; irrigation*
13	20	☆ make offerings; marriage; engagements; funerals; end mourning; hunt and fish; sow crops; install gravestone
F	○	✖ *kitchen work; dig wells; irrigation*
14	21	☆ make offerings; repair paths; paint walls; demolish old house; travel; install roof
S	○	✖ *hairstyling; manicure babies; funerals*
15	22	☆ make offerings; new clothes; hairstyling; baths; business; lay foundations; adopt pets
S	○	✖ *buy houses; prepare wedding bed*

● lucky day   ○ neutral day   ●unlucky day   ❐ 24 solar terms
☆ auspicious activity   ✖ inauspicious activity

16	23	☆ make offerings; pray for happiness; engagements; marriage; new clothes; hairstyling; adopt pets; funerals
M	●	✖ lay foundations; end mourning
17	24	☆ make offerings; baths; demolish old house unlucky day: no important activities
T	●	✖ repair fishing nets; open stores
18	25	☆ demolish old house/wall unlucky day: no important activities
W	●	✖ marriage; make wine
19	26	☆ make offerings; pray for happiness; study; visit friends; engagements; marriage; install roof
T	●	✖ irrigation; drain water; christen boat
20	27	☆ make offerings; receive payment; adopt pets; install furnaces; hunt ❏ Grain Rain
F	○	✖ legal trial; dig wells; deliver goods
21	28	☆ study; visit friends; open stores; irrigation; dig wells; end mourning; buy houses
S	●	✖ make offerings; pray for happiness; acupuncture
22	29	☆ make offerings; pray for happiness; open stores; sign contracts; business; end mourning
S	○	✖ sow crops; dig wells; dig ponds
23	1st	☆ make offerings; hunt and fish; paint walls; funerals; repair fishing nets; prepare wedding bed
M	○	✖ lay foundations; install furnaces; marriage; move house
24	2	☆ make offerings; pray for happiness; pray for fertility; visit friends; engagements; marriage; move house
T	●	✖ hairstyling; travel; end mourning
25	3	☆ travel; visit friends; hunt and fish; sow crops hairstyling; new clothes; open stores
W	○	✖ buy house/land; funerals; marriage
26	4	☆ hairstyling; hunt and fish; travel; install gravestone; repair paths; paint walls
T	○	✖ move house; medical check
27	5	☆ make offerings; baths; new clothes; adopt pets; end mourning; funerals; install door
F	○	✖ repair fishing nets; prepare wedding bed
28	6	☆ make offerings; pray for happiness; baths; hairstyling; manicure babies; medical check; end mourning; funerals
S	●	✖ make preserves; lay foundations
29	7	☆ medical check; demolish old house unlucky day: no important activities
S	●	✖ christen boat; drain water
30	8	☆ repair fishing nets; demolish houses unlucky day: no important activities
M	●	✖ legal trial; marriage; funerals

● lucky day   ○ neutral day   ● unlucky day   ❏ 24 solar terms
☆ auspicious activity   ✖ inauspicious activity

1	9	☆ make offerings; pray for happiness; study; visit friends; open stores; sign contracts
T	●	✖ *lay foundations; new clothes; legal trial*
2	10	☆ marriage; engagements; receive payment; hunt and fish; adopt pets; buy houses
W	○	✖ *sow crops; dig wells*
3	11	☆ study; visit friends; travel; engagements; move house; lay foundations; buy houses
T	●	✖ *kitchen work; make offerings; pray for happiness*
4	12	☆ make offerings; paint walls unlucky day: no important activities
F	●	✖ *hairstyling; dig wells*
5	13	☆ make offerings; visit friends; paint walls; install roof ❏ Beginning of Summer
S	○	✖ *lay foundations; buy houses/terrain*
6	14	☆ repair fishing nets; receive payment; disinfection; funerals; install roof
S	○	✖ *travel; lay foundations*
7	15	☆ make offerings; pray for happiness; visit friends; travel; marriage; move house; hairstyling; open stores
M	●	✖ *repair fishing nets; bathroom work*
8	16	☆ do-it-yourself; buy houses/terrain; prepare wedding bed; interior decoration; receive payment
T	○	✖ *make preserves; make wine*
9	17	☆ baths; hairstyling; housecleaning; travel; end mourning; repair paths; paint walls; install roof
W	○	✖ *irrigation; prepare wedding bed*
10	18	☆ study; travel; engagements; marriage; move house; hairstyling; open stores
T	●	✖ *legal trial; sow crops; buying houses*
11	19	☆ make offerings; marriage; hairstyling; lay foundations; build dams; prepare wedding bed; hunt
F	●	✖ *install furnaces; move house; deliver goods*
12	20	☆ demolish old house/wall unlucky day: no important activities
S	●	✖ *marriage; end mourning; sow crops*
13	21	☆ make offerings; visit friends; travel; marriage; move house; open stores; lay foundations
S	●	✖ *install furnaces; kitchen work; end mourning*
14	22	☆ study; visit friends; travel; engagements; medical check; open stores
M	●	✖ *hairstyling; manicure babies; legal trial; hunt*
15	23	☆ house building; hunt and fish; repair fishing nets; marriage; engagements
T	○	✖ *lay foundations; make offerings; buy houses*

● lucky day ○ neutral day ●unlucky day ❏ 24 solar terms
☆ auspicious activity ✖ inauspicious activity

198

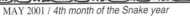

MAY 2001 / 4th month of the Snake year

16	24	☆make offerings; study; visit friends; travel; marriage; hairstyling; prepare wedding bed
W	○	✖ *dig wells; lay foundations*
17	25	☆make offerings; travel; move house; business; lay foundations; funerals
T	●	✖ *repair fishing nets; new clothes*
18	26	☆make offerings; pray for happiness; visit friends; engagements; marriage; new clothes; move house
F	●	✖ *travel; make wine*
19	27	☆make offerings; pray for happiness; visit friends; travel; hairstyling; medical check; funerals; adopt pets
S	●	✖ *irrigation; drain water; end mourning*
20	28	☆sow crops; repair fishing nets; buy houses; paint walls
S	○	✖ *legal trial; funerals*
21	29	☆marriage; engagements; travel; house building; install roof; end mourning ❐ Grain Full
M	○	✖ *prepare wedding bed*
22	30	☆make offerings; pray for happiness; study; travel; marriage; move house; prepare wedding bed
T	◑	✖ *sow crops; christen boat*
23	1st	☆make offerings; pray for happiness; pray for fertility; visit friends; engagements; hairstyling; cut trees
W	○	✖ *kitchen work; mourning*
24	2	☆make offerings; baths; demolish old house; unlucky day: no important activities
T	●	✖ *hairstyling; marriage; move house*
25	3	☆make offerings; pray for happiness; visit friends; travel; marriage; hairstyling; lay foundations; new clothes
F	○	✖ *buying house; christen boat*
26	4	☆make offerings; pray for happiness; study; visit friends; engagements; new clothes; business
S	○	✖ *legal trial; move house; hunt and fish*
27	5	☆visit friends; travel; marriage; move house; business; sign contracts; funerals
S	●	✖ *make offerings; lay foundations*
28	6	☆make offerings; pray for happiness; study; visit friends; travel; business; buy houses
M	●	✖ *make preserves; make wine; dig wells*
29	7	☆repair fishing nets; hunt and fish; medical check; dig wells; irrigation; install roof
T	○	✖ *make preserves; dig wells; move house*
30	8	☆visit friends; new clothes; hunt and fish; paint walls; funerals
W	○	✖ *legal trial; lay foundations; travel*
31	9	☆make offerings; pray for happiness; visit friends; travel; adopt pets; install roof; funerals
T	●	✖ *bathroom work; deliver goods; payment*

● lucky day ○neutral day ◑unlucky day ❐ 24 solar terms
☆ auspicious activity ✖ inauspicious activity

JUNE 2001 / 4th month of the Snake year

1	10	☆ make offerings; visit friends; engagements; receive payment; kitchen work; new clothes
F	○	✘ *open stores; funerals; paint walls*
2	11	☆ visit friends; travel; marriage; move house; open stores; sign contracts; lay foundations
S	●	✘ *install furnaces; prepare wedding bed*
3	12	☆ travel; engagements; marriage; move house; open stores; business; funerals
S	●	✘ *hairstyling; manicure babies; christen boat*
4	13	☆ make offerings; pray for happiness; marriage; move house; hairstyling; construction; lay foundations; mourning
M	●	✘ *buy house/land; do-it-yourself*
5	14	☆ demolish old house unlucky day: no important activities ❑ Grain in Ear
T	●	✘ *marriage; end mourning*
6	15	☆ demolish old house; baths; hunt fish; unlucky day: no important activities
W	●	✘ *repair fishing nets; install furnaces*
7	16	☆ make offerings; pray for happiness; visit friends; marriage; open stores; irrigation
T	○	✘ *make preserves; make wine*
8	17	☆ study; visit friends; travel; engagements; marriage; hairstyling; open stores; funerals
F	●	✘ *irrigation; drain water; make offerings*
9	18	☆ make offerings; hunt and fish; prepare wedding bed; repair fishing nets
S	○	✘ *legal trial; dig wells*
10	19	☆ make offerings; pray for happiness; study; visit friends; engagements; move house; install roof
S	○	✘ *lay foundations; deliver goods*
11	20	☆ do-it-yourself; new clothes; install roof unlucky day: no important activities
M	●	✘ *sow crops; travel*
12	21	☆ make offerings; new clothes; end mourning; prepare wedding bed
T	○	✘ *install furnaces; lay foundations; marriage*
13	22	☆ make offerings; pray for happiness; visit friends; travel; marriage; new clothes; move house
W	●	✘ *hairstyling; end mourning; funeral*
14	23	☆ make offerings; pray for happiness; travel; marriage; new clothes; move house; hairstyling; lay foundations
T	●	✘ *buy house/land; prepare wedding bed*
15	24	☆ hairstyling; housecleaning; demolish old house; repair paths; paint walls
F	●	✘ *kitchen work; marriage; funerals*

● lucky day ○ neutral day ● unlucky day ❑ 24 solar terms
☆ auspicious activity ✘ inauspicious activity

200

16	25	☆make offerings; pray for happiness; study; visit friends; travel; marriage; move house; funerals
S	●	✖ *repair fishing nets; acupuncture*
17	26	☆make offerings; move house; install roof
		unlucky day: no important activities
S	●	✖ *marriage; make wine*
18	27	☆demolish old house/wall
		unlucky day: no important activities
M	●	✖ *irrigation; drain water*
19	28	☆make offerings; open stores; business; construction; lay foundations; paint walls
T	○	✖ *legal trial; end mourning*
20	29	☆demolish old house
		unlucky day: no important activities
W	●	✖ *make offerings; deliver goods*
21	1st	☆ prepare wedding bed; hunt and fish
		unlucky day: no important activities ❑ Summer Solstice
T	●	✖ *dig wells; christen boat*
22	2	☆make offerings; study; visit friends; travel; marriage; move house; lay foundations
F	●	✖ *kitchen work; cut trees*
23	3	☆new clothes; build dams; paint walls; lay foundations; install furnaces; dig ponds
S	○	✖ *hairstyling; travel; mourning*
24	4	☆make offerings; funerals
S	○	✖ *buy houses; lay foundations*
25	5	☆visit friends; travel; move house; hairstyling; open stores; lay foundations; funerals
M	●	✖ *legal trial; end mourning*
26	6	☆make offerings; pray for happiness; travel; construction; hairstyling; new clothes; open stores; lay foundations
T	●	✖ *repair fishing nets; prepare wedding bed*
27	7	☆hairstyling; housecleaning; repair paths; paint walls
W	○	✖ *make preserves; make wine*
28	8	☆make offerings; visit friends; travel; marriage; new clothes; move house; business
T	●	✖ *irrigation; lay foundations; sow crops*
29	9	☆make offerings; pray for happiness; travel; marriage
		unlucky day: no important activities
F	●	✖ *legal trial; marriage; engagements*
30	10	☆medical check; demolish old house/wall
		unlucky day: no important activities
S	●	✖ *deliver goods; payment*

● lucky day ○ neutral day ●unlucky day ❑ 24 solar terms
☆ auspicious activity ✖ inauspicious activity

201

JULY 2001 / 5th month of the Snake year

1 S	11 ○	☆ make offerings; hairstyling; lay foundations; irrigation; visit friends; move house; dig wells; funerals ✖ christen boat; buy houses
2 M	12 ●	☆ study; visit friends; travel; engagements; marriage; open stores; business ✖ kitchen work; make offerings; pray for happiness
3 T	13 ○	☆ make offerings; new clothes; install roof; visits friends ✖ hairstyling; dig wells; funerals
4 W	14 ●	☆ make offerings; pray for happiness; study; visit friends; move house; engagements; lay foundations ✖ buy house/land; cut trees
5 T	15 ●	☆ Lunar Eclipse unlucky day: no important activities ✖ travel; end mourning
6 F	16 ○	☆ paint walls; repair paths; new clothes; prepare wedding bed; funerals ✖ repair fishing nets; lay foundations
7 S	17 ●	☆ travel; engagements; open stores; new clothes; install roof ❏ Slight Heat ✖ make preserves; make wine
8 S	18 ○	☆ make offerings; pray for happiness; hairstyling; open stores; medical check; funerals ✖ irrigation; prepare wedding bed
9 M	19 ○	☆ make offerings; marriage; baths; install furnaces; funerals; cut trees; baths; housecleaning ✖ legal trial; acupuncture
10 T	20 ○	☆ marriage; install furnaces; repair fishing nets; paint walls ✖ payment; deliver goods
11 W	21 ●	☆ hairstyling; buy houses; demolish old house/wall unlucky day: no important activities ✖ marriage; mourning
12 T	22 ○	☆ make offerings; hairstyling; manicure babies; dig wells new clothes ✖ kitchen work; install furnaces; marriage
13 F	23 ●	☆ demolish old house/wall unlucky day: no important activities ✖ hairstyling; open stores; travel
14 S	24 ●	☆ engagements; travel; visit friends; prepare wedding bed; sign contracts; install furnaces ✖ buy house/land; make offerings; pray for happiness
15 S	25 ●	☆ make offerings; pray for happiness; visit friends; open stores; study; lay foundations ✖ dig wells/ponds; end mourning

● lucky day   ○ neutral day   ●unlucky day   ❏ 24 solar terms
☆ auspicious activity   ✖ inauspicious activity

202

JULY 2001 / 6th month of the Snake year

16 M	26 ○	☆ make offerings; receive payment; visit friends; lay foundations; sow crops; move house ❑ *1st Dog Days period* ✖ *repair fishing nets; funerals*
17 T	27 ○	☆ make offerings; study; visit friends; hairstyling; prepare wedding bed; medical check ✖ *make preserves; make wine*
18 W	28 ○	☆ mourning; funerals; end mourning; install roof; do-it-yourself ✖ *irrigation; drain water*
19 T	29 ○	☆ make offerings; visit friends; marriage; move house; open stores; install roof ✖ *legal trial; lay foundations*
20 F	30 ●	☆ make offerings; study; open stores; construction; lay foundations; funerals ✖ *prepare wedding bed; christen boat*
21 S	1st ○	☆ make offerings; baths; lay foundations; open stores; install furnaces; end mourning; funerals ✖ *sow crops; construction; acupuncture*
22 S	2 ○	☆ make offerings; new clothes; install roof repair fishing nets; hunt and fish ✖ *install furnaces; lay foundations*
23 M	3 ●	☆ demolish old house/wall; baths; housecleaning; unlucky day: no important activities ❑ *Great Heat* ✖ *hairstyling; marriage; mourning*
24 T	4 ○	☆ make offerings; travel; hairstyling; manicure babies; new clothes; repair fishing nets; hunt and fish ✖ *buy house/land; visit fortuneteller*
25 W	5 ●	☆ make offerings; medical check; demolish old house/wall unlucky day: no important activities ✖ *end mourning; mourning*
26 T	6 ●	☆ study; visit friends; travel; engagements; hairstyling; open stores; business ❑ *2nd Dog Days period* ✖ *repair fishing nets; install furnaces; make offerings*
27 F	7 ●	☆ make offerings; pray for happiness; visit friends; travel; marriage; move house; open stores ✖ *make preserves; make wine; dig wells*
28 S	8 ○	☆ receive payment; hunt and fish; prepare wedding bed; sow crops; medical check ✖ *irrigation; drain water*
29 S	9 ○	☆ study; visit friends; engagements; hairstyling; prepare wedding bed; new clothes ✖ *legal trial; travel*
30 M	10 ●	☆ make offerings; make wine; make preserves; do-it-yourself; funerals ✖ *buy goods; deliver goods*
31 T	11 ●	☆ travel; marriage; open stores; business; prepare wedding bed; adopt pets ✖ *sow crops; lay foundations*

● lucky day　○ neutral day　● unlucky day　　❑ 24 solar terms
☆ auspicious activity　✖ inauspicious activity

203

1 W ●	12	☆ baths; open stores; business; install roof; mourning; funerals ✖ *kitchen work; prepare wedding bed*
2 T ●	13	☆ baths; sign contracts; business; lay foundations; install roof; funerals ✖ *hairstyling; paint walls; acupuncture*
3 F ○	14	☆ marriage; engagements; repair fishing nets ✖ *lay foundations; buy houses*
4 S ●	15	☆ make offerings; hairstyling unlucky day: no important activities ✖ *marriage; end mourning*
5 S ○	16	☆ pray for happiness; study; travel; new clothes; baths; hairstyling; prepare wedding bed ✖ *repair fishing nets; visit fortuneteller*
6 M ●	17	☆ demolish old house/wall unlucky day: no important activities ✖ *make preserves; make wine*
7 T ●	18	☆ visit friends; travel; engagements; move house; baths; housecleaning ❑ Beginning of Autumn ✖ *irrigation; make offerings; pray for happiness*
8 W ●	19	☆ make offerings; pray for happiness; study; visit friends; sign contracts; business ✖ *legal trial; lay foundations; dig wells; dig ponds*
9 T ○	20	☆ make offerings; pray for happiness; study; visit friends; sign contracts; business ✖ *end mourning; payment*
10 F ●	21	☆ hairstyling; baths; hunt and fish; housecleaning unlucky day: no important activities ✖ *sow crops; travel*
11 S ●	22	☆ make offerings; pray for happiness; study; travel; engagements; open stores; lay foundations ✖ *kitchen work; install furnaces*
12 S ○	23	☆ make offerings; study; engagements; move house; lay foundations; build dams ✖ *hairstyling; manicure babies; acupuncture*
13 M ●	24	☆ make offerings; pray for happiness; visit friends; travel; marriage; move house; hairstyling; funerals ✖ *buy houses; prepare wedding bed*
14 T ○	25	☆ make offerings; hairstyling; new clothes; lay foundations; install roof; mourning; funerals ✖ *do-it-yourself; hunt and fish*
15 W ○	26	☆ visit friends; hairstyling; new clothes; sow crops; adopt pets ❑ 3rd Dog Days period ✖ *repair fishing nets*

● lucky day ○ neutral day ● unlucky day ❑ 24 solar terms
☆ auspicious activity ✖ inauspicious activity

204

AUGUST 2001 / 7th month of the Snake year

16	27	☆ demolish old house unlucky day: no important activities
T	●	✖ *make preserves; marriage*
17	28	☆ make offerings; pray for happiness; study; visit friends; travel; engagements; marriage; funerals
F	●	✖ *dig wells; drain water; visit fortuneteller*
18	29	☆ make offerings; pray for happiness; visit friends; travel; engagements; new clothes; lay foundations; funerals
S	●	✖ *legal trial; move house*
19	1st	☆ demolish old house/wall unlucky day: no important activities
S	●	✖ *make offerings; deliver goods*
20	2	☆ make offerings; pray for fertility; visit friends; marriage; hairstyling; prepare wedding bed; funerals
M	○	✖ *lay foundations; dig wells; dig ponds*
21	3	☆ make offerings; pray for happiness; study; engagements; new clothes; open stores; sign contracts
T	○	✖ *kitchen work; acupuncture*
22	4	☆ make offerings; pray for fertility; visit friends; engagements; marriage; move house; open stores
W	●	✖ *hairstyling; travel*
23	5	☆ visit friends; travel; marriage; move house; open stores ❑ Limit of Heat
T	●	✖ *buy house/land; bathroom work*
24	6	☆ engagements; irrigation; lay foundations
F	○	✖ *kitchen work; install furnaces*
25	7	☆ travel; new clothes; install door; install furnaces; house building; adopt pets
S	●	✖ *prepare wedding bed; lay foundations*
26	8	☆ make offerings; baths; lay foundations; install roof; install furnaces; irrigation; end mourning; funerals
S	○	✖ *make preserves; make wine; hunt and fish*
27	9	☆ visit friends; travel; marriage; move house; open stores; business
M	●	✖ *irrigation; drain water; end mourning*
28	10	☆ repair paths; housecleaning unlucky day: no important activities
T	●	✖ *legal trial; marriage*
29	11	☆ make offerings; pray for happiness; visit friends; travel; engagements; move house; lay foundations
W	●	✖ *end mourning; deliver goods; payment*
30	12	☆ visit friends; hunt and fish; adopt pets
T	○	✖ *christen boat; sow crops*
31	13	☆ medical check; demolish old house; unlucky day: no important activities
F	●	✖ *install furnaces; make offerings*

● lucky day   ○ neutral day   ● unlucky day   ❑ 24 solar terms
☆ auspicious activity   ✖ inauspicious activity

SEPTEMBER 2001 / 8th month of the Snake year

1 S	*14* ●	☆ make offerings; pray for happiness; visit friends; travel; marriage; move house; business ✖ *hairstyling; dig wells; lay foundations*
2 S	*15* ●	☆ make offerings; visit friends; travel; engagements; new clothes; open stores; lay foundations ✖ *buy house/land; acupuncture*
3 M	*16* ●	☆ make offerings; visit friends; marriage; move house; open stores; lay foundations ✖ *travel; mourning*
4 T	*17* ○	☆ study; travel; visit friends; engagements; open stores; lay foundations ✖ *repair fishing nets; bathroom work*
5 W	*18* ○	☆ travel; new clothes; lay foundations; install roof; prepare wedding bed ✖ *make preserves; make wine*
6 T	*19* ●	☆ make offerings; pray for happiness; visit friends; travel; marriage; move house; hairstyling; funerals ✖ *irrigation; prepare wedding bed; lay foundations*
7 F	*20* ●	☆ engagements; hairstyling; lay foundations; mourning; funerals ❑ White Dew ✖ *legal trial; do-it-yourself*
8 S	*21* ○	☆ travel; hairstyling; move house; sow crops; housecleaning; prepare wedding bed; irrigation ✖ *buy goods; payment; deliver goods*
9 S	*22* ●	☆ make offerings; cut trees unlucky day: no important activities ✖ *marriage; mourning*
10 M	*23* ○	☆ repair paths; paint walls ✖ *kitchen work; install furnaces*
11 T	*24* ●	☆ study; visit friends; engagements; marriage; new clothes; move house; lay foundations ✖ *hairstyling; manicure babies; interior decoration*
12 W	*25* ○	☆ engagements; hairstyling; lay foundations; install roof; end mourning; funerals ✖ *buy houses; make offerings*
13 T	*26* ●	☆ demolish old house/wall unlucky day: no important activities ✖ *dig wells; dig ponds*
14 F	*27* ●	☆ make offerings; pray for happiness; visit friends; travel; marriage; move house; open stores ✖ *repair fishing nets; fishing; travel*
15 S	*28* ●	☆ make offerings; pray for happiness; study; visit friends; marriage; move house; lay foundations ✖ *make preserves; make wine; travel; end mourning*

● lucky day   ○ neutral day   ● unlucky day   ❑ 24 solar terms
☆ auspicious activity   ✖ inauspicious activity

206

16	29	☆ hairstyling; hunt and fish; adopt pets
S	○	✗ *irrigation; drain water*
17	1st	☆ make offerings; pray for happiness/fertility; study; visit friends; travel; marriage; new clothes; end mourning
M	●	✗ *legal trial; lay foundations*
18	2	☆ make offerings; travel; hairstyling; marriage; move house; business; lay foundations; funerals
T	●	✗ *prepare wedding bed; deliver goods*
19	3	☆ baths; travel; housecleaning; buy houses; interior decoration
W	○	✗ *sow crops; lay foundations*
20	4	☆ make offerings; travel; hairstyling; lay foundations; medical check; housecleaning; prepare wedding bed
T	○	✗ *install furnaces; funerals*
21	5	☆ housecleaning; cut trees — unlucky day: no important activities
F	●	✗ *hairstyling; marriage*
22	6	☆ make offerings — unlucky day: no important activities
S	●	✗ *buy house/land*
23	7	☆ visit friends; marriage; move house; open stores; lay foundations ◻ Autumn Equinox
S	●	✗ *sow crops; christen boat*
24	8	☆ study; travel; engagements; hairstyling; lay foundations; funerals
M	○	✗ *repair fishing nets; make offerings*
25	9	☆ demolish old house/wall — unlucky day: no important activities
T	●	✗ *make preserves; dig wells*
26	10	☆ make offerings; pray for happiness; study; travel; marriage; new clothes; move house; funerals
W	○	✗ *irrigation; drain water*
27	11	☆ make offerings; pray for happiness; study; visit friends; travel; marriage; install roof
T	○	✗ *legal trial; travel; christen boat*
28	12	☆ marriage; hunt and fish; hairstyling
F	○	✗ *deliver goods*
29	13	☆ make offerings; pray for happiness; study; visit friends; travel; marriage; move house; new clothes
S	●	✗ *lay foundations; mourning*
30	14	☆ make offerings; travel; hairstyling; new clothes; house building; drain water; funerals
S	●	✗ *kitchen work; prepare wedding bed*

● lucky day ○ neutral day ● unlucky day ◻ 24 solar terms
☆ auspicious activity ✗ inauspicious activity

207

OCTOBER 2001 / 10th month of the Snake year

1	15	☆ make offerings; funerals; cut trees
		❏ Middle-Autumn Festival
M	○	✖ *hairstyling; lay foundations*
2	16	☆ travel; hairstyling; medical check; lay foundations; prepare wedding bed
T	●	✖ *buy houses; funerals*
3	17	☆ make offerings; demolish old house/wall; cut trees
		unlucky day: no important activities
W	●	✖ *marriage; mourning*
4	18	☆ repair paths; paint walls
T	○	✖ *repair fishing nets; see fortuneteller*
5	19	☆ travel; visit friends; hairstyling; move house; prepare wedding bed; adopt pets
F	●	✖ *make preserves; make wine; end mourning*
6	20	☆ study; visit friends; travel; hairstyling; install furnaces; sow crops; funerals
S	○	✖ *irrigation; make offerings; pray for happiness*
7	21	☆ medical check; demolish old house
		unlucky day: no important activities
S	●	✖ *legal trial; dig wells*
8	22	☆ sow crops; open stores; move house; prepare wedding bed ❏ Cold Dew
M	○	✖ *deliver goods; payment; travel in boat*
9	23	☆ make offerings; housecleaning
		unlucky day: no important activities
T	●	✖ *sow crops; travel*
10	24	☆ make offerings; pray for happiness/fertility; study; visit friends; travel; marriage; move house
W	●	✖ *kitchen work; install furnaces; bathroom work*
11	25	☆ adopt pets; hunt and fish; repair fishing nets
T	○	✖ *hairstyling; manicure babies*
12	26	☆ make offerings; pray for happiness; study; travel; marriage; move house; hairstyling; lay foundations
F	●	✖ *buy house/land; prepare wedding bed*
13	27	☆ baths; hairstyling; lay foundations; build dams; sow crops; install furnaces; funerals
S	○	✖ *end mourning;*
14	28	☆ make offerings; visit friends; travel; move house; receive payment; install roof
S	●	✖ *lay foundations; end mourning; repair fishing nets*
15	29	☆ make offerings; cut trees
		unlucky day: no important activities
M	●	✖ *marriage*

●lucky day ○neutral day ●unlucky day ❏ 24 solar terms
☆auspicious activity ✖ inauspicious activity

16	30	☆	make offerings; study; visit friends; travel; hairstyling; open stores; sign contracts
T	○	✖	*irrigation; drain water; visit fortuneteller*
17	1st	☆	do-it-yourself; kitchen work
W	○	✖	*legal trial; christen boat*
18	2	☆	visit friends; new clothes; paint walls; funerals
T	○	✖	*make offerings; payment; deliver goods*
19	3	☆	make offerings; pray for happiness; prepare wedding bed; repair fishing nets
F	○	✖	*dig wells; dig ponds; christen boat*
20	4	☆	make offerings; demolish old house/wall; unlucky day: no important activities
S	●	✖	*kitchen work*
21	5	☆	make offerings; engagements; prepare wedding bed; adopt pets
S	○	✖	*hairstyling; travel*
22	6	☆	study; visit friends; travel; engagements; marriage; move house; hairstyling; lay foundations
M	●	✖	*buy house/land; bathroom work*
23	7	☆	adopt pets; hunt and fish ❐ First Frost
T	○	✖	*christen boat; end mourning*
24	8	☆	make offerings; pray for happiness; study; travel; move house; hairstyling; buy houses; sow crops
W	●	✖	*repair fishing nets; prepare wedding bed*
25	9	☆	make offerings; hairstyling; new clothes; prepare wedding bed; mourning; funerals ❐ Double 9 Festival
T	○	✖	*make preserves; make wine; acupuncture*
26	10	☆	make offerings; pray for happiness; visit friends; engagements; prepare wedding bed; construction
F	●	✖	*irrigation; lay foundations; drain water*
27	11	☆	demolish old house/wall; disinfection unlucky day: no important activities
S	●	✖	*legal trial; marriage*
28	12	☆	study; visit friends; travel; open stores; receive payment; end mourning
S	○	✖	*deliver goods; christen boat*
29	13	☆	make offerings; install furnaces; repair paths; paint walls
M	○	✖	*sow crops*
30	14	☆	visit friends; lay foundations; end mourning; funerals
T	○	✖	*install furnaces; make offerings*
31	15	☆	make offerings; pray for happiness; visit friends; travel; engagements; marriage; lay foundations; funerals
W	●	✖	*hairstyling; manicure babies; dig wells/ponds*

● lucky day ○ neutral day ● unlucky day ❐ 24 solar terms
☆ auspicious activity ✖ inauspicious activity

209

1 T	16 ●	☆ demolish old house/wall unlucky day: no important activities ✘ buy houses/land
2 F	17 ○	☆ make offerings; marriage; prepare wedding bed; lay foundations; adopt an enfant ✘ travel; mourning
3 S	18 ●	☆ make offerings; pray for happiness; pray for fertility; study; engagements; marriage; install furnaces ✘ repair fishing nets; bathroom work
4 S	19 ○	☆ make offerings; marriage; receive payment ✘ lay foundations; make wine
5 M	20 ●	☆ make offerings; pray for happiness; study; travel; move house; hairstyling; buy houses ✘ irrigation; prepare wedding bed; kitchen work
6 T	21 ●	☆ paint walls; housecleaning; hairstyling unlucky day: no important activities ✘ legal trial; do-it-yourself
7 W	22 ○	☆ make offerings; hunt and fish; prepare wedding bed; medical check ❏ Beginning of Winter ✘ funerals; lay foundations
8 T	23 ●	☆ make offerings; baths; demolish old house/wall unlucky day: no important activities ✘ marriage; lay foundations; sow crops
9 F	24 ●	☆ travel; hairstyling; engagements; open stores; business; funerals ✘ kitchen work; install furnaces; visit fortuneteller;
10 S	25 ○	☆ make offerings; visit friends; do-it-yourself; new clothes ✘ hairstyling; funerals
11 S	26 ●	☆ visit friends; travel; engagements; marriage; new clothes; move house; funerals ✘ buying houses; make offerings; lay foundations
12 M	27 ●	☆ make offerings; pray for happiness; study; visit friends; travel; marriage; move house; funerals ✘ dig wells; dig ponds; hunt and fish
13 T	28 ●	☆ visit friends; new clothes; engagements; marriage; adoption; move house; hairstyling; install furnaces ✘ repair fishing nets; lay foundations
14 W	29 ●	☆ medical check; demolish old house unlucky day: no important activities ✘ make preserves; make wine
15 T	1st ○	☆ make offerings; visit friends; engagements; hairstyling; adoption; move house; prepare wedding bed ✘ irrigation; bathroom work

● lucky day   ○ neutral day   ● unlucky day   ❏ 24 solar terms
 ☆ auspicious activity   ✘ inauspicious activity

16 F	2 ●	☆ make offerings; visit friends; engagements; lay foundations; install roof; funerals; adopt pets ✖ *legal trial; install furnaces; kitchen work*
17 S	3 ●	☆ travel; marriage; move house; lay foundations; install roof; funerals ✖ *prepare wedding bed*
18 S	4 ●	☆ make offerings; pray for happiness; study; travel; marriage; move house; hairstyling; new clothes ✖ *sow crops; do-it-yourself*
19 M	5 ○	☆ make offerings; new clothes; build dams; bathroom work; prepare wedding bed ✖ *kitchen work; end mourning*
20 T	6 ●	☆ make offerings; baths; demolish old house/wall ✖ *hairstyling; marriage*
21 W	7 ○	☆ study; travel; hairstyling; open stores; business; lay foundations; housecleaning ✖ *buy house/land; visit fortuneteller*
22 T	8 ○	☆ visit friends; new clothes; lay foundations; open stores; do-it-yourself ❑ Slight Snow ✖ *end mourning; funerals*
23 F	9 ●	☆ travel; marriage; move house; open stores; lay foundations; funerals ✖ *repair fishing nets; make offerings*
24 S	10 ◐	☆ study; visit friends; travel; engagements; marriage; hairstyling; move house; lay foundations ✖ *make preserves; make wine*
25 S	11 ○	☆ study; marriage; hairstyling; medical check; repair fishing nets; hunt and fish ✖ *lay foundations; irrigation*
26 M	12 ●	☆ medical check; demolish old house unlucky day: no important activities ✖ *legal trial; travel*
27 T	13 ●	☆ make offerings; pray for happiness; visit friends; travel; marriage; move house; business ✖ *deliver goods; bathroom work*
28 W	14 ●	☆ make offerings; pray for happiness; study; visit friends; engagements; prepare wedding bed ✖ *sow crops; hunt and fish*
29 T	15 ○	☆ disinfection; housecleaning; repair fishing nets ✖ *install furnaces; prepare wedding bed*
30 F	16 ●	☆ study; travel; move house; open stores; lay foundations; install roof ✖ *hairstyling; manicure babies*

● lucky day ○ neutral day ◐ unlucky day ❑ 24 solar terms
☆ auspicious activity ✖ inauspicious activity

DECEMBER 2001 / 12th month of the Snake year

1	17	☆	construction; lay foundations; bathroom work; repair fishing nets
S	○	✖	*buy house/land*
2	18	☆	hairstyling; demolish old house/wall
			unlucky day: no important activities
S	●	✖	*marriage; lay foundations*
3	19	☆	visit friends; travel; marriage; move house; lay foundations; medical check; funerals
M	●	✖	*repair fishing nets; visit fortuneteller*
4	20	☆	visit friends; hairstyling; do-it-yourself; interior decoration
T	○	✖	*make preserves; make wine; funerals*
5	21	☆	visit friends; travel; marriage; move house; open stores; lay foundations; make wine
W	●	✖	*irrigation; make offerings; drain water*
6	22	☆	make offerings; visit friends; travel; engagements; marriage; move house; hairstyling; funerals
T	●	✖	*legal trial; sow crops; dig wells*
7	23	☆	travel; marriage; move house; open stores; lay foundations ❑ Great Snow
F	●	✖	*christen boat; deliver goods*
8	24	☆	make offerings; housecleaning
			unlucky day: no important activities
S	●	✖	*sow crops; travel*
9	25	☆	demolish old house/wall
			unlucky day: no important activities
S	●	✖	*kitchen work; install furnaces*
10	26	☆	make offerings; engagements; prepare wedding bed; sign contracts; business
M	○	✖	*hairstyling; end mourning*
11	27	☆	study; visit friends; travel; engagements; marriage; move house; mourning; funerals
T	●	✖	*buy house/land; prepare wedding bed*
12	28	☆	baths; hairstyling; receive payment; repair fishing nets
W	○	✖	*kitchen work; install furnaces*
13	29	☆	make offerings; pray for happiness; study; visit friends; marriage; open stores; lay foundations
T	●	✖	*repair fishing nets; cut trees*
14	30	☆	demolish old house/wall
			unlucky day: no important activities
F	●	✖	*make preserves; marriage*
15	1st	☆	Lunar Eclipse
			unlucky day: no important activities
S	○	✖	*irrigation; lay foundations*

● lucky day ○ neutral day ● unlucky day ❑ 24 solar terms
☆ auspicious activity ✖ inauspicious activity

16 S ●	*2*	☆ make offerings; pray for happiness; visit friends; travel; marriage; move house; hairstyling; install furnaces ✘ *legal trial; end mourning; funerals*
17 M ●	*3*	☆ study; visit friends; travel; new clothes; lay foundations; prepare wedding bed ✘ *make offerings; pray for happiness; payment; funerals*
18 T ○	*4*	☆ repair paths; paint walls ✘ *dig wells; dig ponds*
19 W ●	*5*	☆ make offerings; pray for happiness; visit friends; travel; engagements; marriage; business; funerals ✘ *kitchen work; install furnaces; new clothes*
20 T ○	*6*	☆ make offerings; buy houses; interior decoration; hunt and fish ✘ *hairstyling; travel*
21 F ●	*7*	☆ demolish old house/wall unlucky day: no important activities ✘ *buy house/land*
22 S ○	*8*	☆ hairstyling; prepare wedding bed; lay foundations; construction ❒ Winter Solstice ✘ *medical check; travel in boat*
23 S ●	*9*	☆ make offerings; study; visit friends; travel; new clothes; hairstyling; open stores; funerals ✘ *prepare wedding bed; repair fishing nets*
24 M ○	*10*	☆ baths; hairstyling; new clothes; repair fishing nets; receive payment ✘ *lay foundations; make wine*
25 T ●	*11*	☆ make offerings; pray for happiness; study; visit friends; engagements; open stores; buy houses ✘ *irrigation; drain water*
26 W ●	*12*	☆ cut trees; do-it-yourself; housecleaning unlucky day: no important activities ✘ *legal trial; marriage*
27 T ○	*13*	☆ hairstyling; sign contracts; business ✘ *lay foundations; deliver goods*
28 F ●	*14*	☆ make offerings; pray for happiness; visit friends; travel; engagements; marriage; move house; lay foundations ✘ *sow crops; end mourning; funerals*
29 S ●	*15*	☆ study; visit friends; travel; new clothes; open stores; business; funerals ✘ *kitchen work; make offerings; pray for happiness*
30 S ○	*16*	☆ repair paths; paint walls ✘ *hairstyling; dig wells*
31 M ●	*17*	☆ make offerings; pray for happiness; study; visit friends; travel; marriage; prepare wedding bed ✘ *buy house/land; sow crops*

● lucky day ○ neutral day ● unlucky day ❒ 24 solar terms
☆ auspicious activity ✘ inauspicious activity

1	18	☆ buy house; lay foundations; construction; install roof; install furnaces
T	○	✖ *travel; end mourning*
2	19	☆ medical check; demolish old house unlucky day: no important activities
W	●	✖ *repair fishing nets; bathroom work*
3	20	☆ sign contracts; business; prepare wedding bed; mourning
T	○	✖ *make preserves; make wine*
4	21	☆ make offerings; pray for happiness; study; visit friends; travel; marriage; install furnaces; funerals
F	●	✖ *prepare wedding bed; lay foundations*
5	22	☆ receive payment; hunt and fish; hairstyling; sow crops ❑ Slight Cold
S	○	✖ *legal trial; end mourning*
6	23	☆ make offerings; repair fishing nets; install furnaces; sow crops
S	○	✖ *payment; deliver goods*
7	24	☆ make offerings; demolish old house/wall; housecleaning unlucky day: no important activities
M	●	✖ *sow crops; marriage*
8	25	☆ make offerings; new clothes; sign contracts; business; end mourning; funerals
T	○	✖ *kitchen work*
9	26	☆ make offerings; sign contracts
W	○	✖ *hairstyling; funerals*
10	27	☆ study; engagements; marriage; open stores; sign contracts; install furnaces
T	●	✖ *buy house/land; make offerings; pray for happiness*
11	28	☆ make offerings; study; engagements; open stores; business
F	●	✖ *dig wells; dig ponds*
12	29	☆ marriage; repair paths; paint walls
S	○	✖ *repair fishing nets; hunt and fish*
13	1st	☆ make offerings; visit friends; engagements; move house; business; lay foundations
S	●	✖ *make preserves; make wine; end mourning*
14	2	☆ make offerings; travel; hairstyling; lay foundations; prepare wedding bed; funerals
M	●	✖ *irrigation; drain water*
15	3	☆ make offerings; demolish old house/wall unlucky day: no important activities
T	●	✖ *legal trial; open stores*

● lucky day ○ neutral day ● unlucky day ❑ 24 solar terms
☆ auspicious activity ✖ inauspicious activity

16 W ●	4	☆ study; travel; move house; lay foundations; new clothes; adopt pets; funerals ✖ *prepare wedding bed; payment; deliver goods*
17 T ●	5	☆ make offerings; pray for happiness; travel; marriage; move house; open stores ✖ *sow crops; hunt and fish; cut trees*
18 F ○	6	☆ make offerings; receive payment; hunt and fish repair fishing nets ✖ *kitchen work; install furnaces*
19 S ●	7	☆ make offerings; demolish old house/wall unlucky day: no important activities ✖ *hairstyling; marriage*
20 S ○	8	☆ travel; new clothes; hairstyling; prepare wedding bed; open stores ❑ Great Cold ✖ *buy house/land; lay foundations*
21 M ○	9	☆ make offerings; sign contracts; business ✖ *lay foundations; funerals*
22 T ●	10	☆ visit friends; travel; engagements; marriage; move house; new clothes; hairstyling; funerals ✖ *repair fishing nets; install furnaces*
23 W ●	11	☆ make offerings; study; travel; visit friends; marriage; hairstyling; install furnaces; funerals ✖ *make preserves; make wine; dig wells*
24 T ○	12	☆ repair fishing nets; receive payment; funerals ✖ *irrigation*
25 F ●	13	☆ visit friends; engagements; move house; sign contracts ✖ *legal trial; travel; end mourning*
26 S ●	14	☆ make offerings; pray for happiness; travel; hairstyling; new clothes; lay foundations; funerals ✖ *bathroom work*
27 S ●	15	☆ demolish old house/wall unlucky day: no important activities ✖ *sow crops*
28 M ●	16	☆ make offerings; pray for happiness; travel; hairstyling; open stores; business; move house ✖ *kitchen work*
29 T ●	17	☆ make offerings; study; travel; engagements; marriage; move house; lay foundations; install roof ✖ *hairstyling; legal trial; christen boat*
30 W ○	18	☆ make offerings; receive payment; sow crops; hunt and fish ✖ *buy houses; mourning*
31 T ●	19	☆ medical check; demolish old house/wall; unlucky day: no important activities ✖ *marriage; install furnaces*

●lucky day　○neutral day　●unlucky day　❑ 24 solar terms
☆auspicious activity　✖ inauspicious activity

215

1 F	20 ○	☆ make offerings; new clothes; business; prepare wedding bed; funerals ✖ *repair fishing nets; lay foundations*
2 S	21 ●	☆ make offerings; pray for happiness; visit friends; engagements; buy goods; prepare wedding bed ✖ *make preserves; make wine; funerals*
3 S	22 ●	☆ cut trees unlucky day: no important activities ✖ *irrigation; dig wells or ponds*
4 M	23 ●	☆ make offerings; travel; marriage; hairstyling; open stores; funerals ☐ Beginning of Spring ✖ *legal trial; dig wells; christen boat*
5 T	24 ○	☆ make offerings; visit friends; new clothes; repair fishing nets ✖ *deliver goods; funerals*
6 W	25 ○	☆ repair paths; paint walls ✖ *sow crops; travel*
7 T	26 ●	☆ make offerings; pray for happiness; study; visit friends; travel; engagements; open stores ✖ *kitchen work; bathroom work*
8 F	27 ●	☆ make offerings; pray for happiness; travel; move house; lay foundations; install roof ✖ *hairstyling; hunt and fish*
9 S	28 ●	☆ medical check; demolish old house/wall unlucky day: no important activities ✖ *buy houses; prepare wedding bed*
10 S	29 ●	☆ make offerings; pray for happiness; hairstyling; open stores; lay foundations; install roof ✖ *sow crops; do-it-yourself*
11 M	30 ○	☆ make offerings; pray for happiness; study; hairstyling; prepare wedding bed ✖ *end mourning; repair fishing nets*
12 T	1st ●	Year of the Horse begins New Year Happy New Year!

● lucky day ○neutral day ●unlucky day ☐ 24 solar terms
☆ auspicious activity ✖ inauspicious activity

216

Dates of Lunar Years

18.02.1912 to 05.02.1913: RAT
06.02.1913 to 25.01.1914: OX
26.01.1914 to 13.02.1915: TIGER
14.02.1915 to 02.02.1916: RABBIT
03.02.1916 to 22.01.1917: DRAGON
23.01.1917 to 10.02.1918: SNAKE
11.02.1918 to 31.01.1919: HORSE
01.02.1919 to 19.02.1920: RAM
20.02.1920 to 07.02.1921: MONKEY
08.02.1921 to 27.01.1922: ROOSTER
28.01.1922 to 15.02.1923: DOG
16.02.1923 to 04.02.1924: PIG

05.02.1924 to 24.01.1925: RAT
25.01.1925 to 12.02.1926: OX
13.02.1926 to 01.02 1927: TIGER
02.02.1927 to 22.01.1928: RABBIT
23.01.1928 to 09.02.1929: DRAGON
10.02.1929 to 29.01.1930: SNAKE
30.01.1930 to 16.02.1931: HORSE
17.02.1931 to 05.02.1932: RAM
06.02.1932 to 25.01.1933: MONKEY
26.01.1933 to 13.02.1934: ROOSTER
14.02.1934 to 03.02.1935: DOG
04.02.1935 to 23.01.1936: PIG

24.01.1936 to 10.02.1937: RAT
11.02.1937 to 30.01.1938: OX
31.01.1938 to 18.02.1939: TIGER
19.02.1939 to 07.02.1940: RABBIT
08.02.1940 to 26.01.1941: DRAGON
27.01.1941 to 14.02.1942: SNAKE
15.02.1942 to 04.02.1943: HORSE
05.02.1943 to 24.01.1944: RAM
25.01.1944 to 12.02.1945: MONKEY
13.02.1945 to 01.02.1946: ROOSTER
02.02.1946 to 21.01.1947: DOG
22.01.1947 to 09.02.1948: PIG

10.02.1948 to 28.01.1949: RAT
29.01.1949 to 16.02.1950: OX
17.02.1950 to 05.02.1951: TIGER
06.02.1951 to 26.01.1952: RABBIT
27.01.1952 to 13.02.1953: DRAGON
14.02.1953 to 02.02.1954: SNAKE
03.02.1954 to 23.01.1955: HORSE
24.01.1955 to 11.02.1956: RAM
12.02.1956 to 30.01 1957: MONKEY
31.01.1957 to 17.02.1958: ROOSTER
18.02.1958 to 07.02.1959: DOG
08.02.1959 to 27.01.1960: PIG

28.01.1960 to 14.02.1961: RAT
15.02.1961 to 04.02.1962: OX
05.02.1962 to 24.01.1963: TIGER
25.01.1963 to 12.02.1964: RABBIT
13.02.1964 to 01.02.1965: DRAGON
02.02.1965 to 20.01.1966: SNAKE
21.01.1966 to 08.02.1967: HORSE
09.02.1967 to 29.01.1968: RAM
30.01.1968 to 16.02.1969: MONKEY
17.02.1969 to 05.02.1970: ROOSTER
06.02.1970 to 26.01.1971: DOG
27.01.1971 to 14.02.1972: PIG

15.02.1972 to 02.02.1973: RAT
03.02.1973 to 22.01.1974: OX
23.01.1974 to 10.02.1975: TIGER
11.02.1975 to 30.01.1976: RABBIT
31.01.1976 to 17.02.1977: DRAGON
18.02.1977 to 06.02.1978: SNAKE
07.02.1978 to 27.01.1979: HORSE
28.01.1979 to 15.02.1980: RAM
16.02.1980 to 04.02.1981: MONKEY
05.02.1981 to 24.01.1982: ROOSTER
25.01.1982 to 12.02.1983: DOG
13.02.1983 to 01.02.1984: PIG

02.02.1984 to 19.02.1985: RAT
20.02.1985 to 08.02.1986: OX
09.02.1986 to 28.01.1987: TIGER
29.01.1987 to 16.02.1988: RABBIT
17.02.1988 to 05.02.1989: DRAGON
06.02.1989 to 26.01.1990: SNAKE
27.01.1990 to 14.02.1991: HORSE
15.02.1991 to 03.02.1992: RAM
04.02.1992 to 22.01.1993: MONKEY
23.01.1993 to 09.02.1994: ROOSTER
10.02.1994 to 30.01.1995: DOG
31.01.1995 to 18.02.1996: PIG

19.02.1996 to 06.02.1997: RAT
07.02.1997 to 27.01.1998: OX
28.01.1998 to 15.02.1999: TIGER
16.02.1999 to 04.02.2000: RABBIT
05.02.2000 to 23.01.2001: DRAGON
24.01.2001 to 11.02.2002: SNAKE
12.02.2002 to 31.01.2003: HORSE
01.02.2003 to 21.01.2004: RAM
22.01.2004 to 08.02.2005: MONKEY
09.02.2005 to 28.01.2006: ROOSTER
29.01.2006 to 17.02.2007: DOG
18.02.2007 to 06.02.2008: PIG

Predicting the Sex of a Child

12	11	10	9	8	7	6	5	4	3	2	1	Lunar month of conception / Mother's age
M	M	M	M	M	M	M	M	M	F	M	F	18
F	F	M	M	M	M	M	F	F	M	F	M	19
M	M	F	M	M	M	M	M	M	F	M	F	20
F	F	F	F	F	F	F	F	F	F	F	M	21
F	F	F	F	M	F	F	M	F	M	M	F	22
F	M	M	M	F	M	F	M	M	F	M	M	23
F	F	F	F	F	M	M	F	M	M	F	M	24
M	M	M	M	M	F	M	F	F	M	M	F	25
F	F	F	F	M	F	M	F	F	M	F	M	26
M	F	M	M	M	M	F	F	M	F	M	F	27
F	F	M	M	M	M	F	F	F	M	F	M	28
F	F	F	M	M	M	M	M	F	F	M	F	29
M	M	F	F	F	F	F	F	F	F	F	M	30
M	F	F	F	F	F	F	F	F	M	F	M	31
M	F	F	F	F	F	F	F	F	M	F	M	32
M	F	F	F	M	F	F	F	M	F	M	F	33
M	M	F	F	F	F	F	F	F	M	F	M	34
M	M	F	F	M	F	F	F	M	F	M	M	35
M	M	M	M	F	F	F	M	F	M	M	F	36
M	F	M	F	M	F	M	F	M	M	F	M	37
F	M	F	M	F	M	F	M	M	F	M	F	38
F	F	M	F	M	F	F	M	M	M	F	M	39
F	M	F	M	F	M	M	F	M	F	M	F	40
M	F	M	F	M	M	F	M	F	M	F	M	41
F	M	F	M	M	F	M	F	M	F	M	F	42
M	M	M	M	F	M	F	M	F	M	F	M	43
F	F	M	F	M	F	M	M	F	M	M	M	44
M	M	F	M	F	M	F	F	F	M	M	F	45

*Lunar calendar

Months of the Snake Year

Lunar month	Solar date
1st	24 January to 22 February 2001
2nd	23 February to 24 March 2001
3rd	25 March to 22 April 2001
4th	23 April to 22 May 2001
4th supplemental	23 May to 20 June 2001
5th	21 June to 20 July 2001
6th	21 July to 18 August 2001
7th	19 August to 16 September 2001
8th	17 September to 16 October 2001
9th	17 October to 14 November 2001
10th	15 November to 14 December 2001
11th	15 December to 12 January 2001
12th	13 January 2001 to 11 February 2002